China in Revolution

From a painting in the Whampoa Military Academy

THE SHAKEE-SHAMEEN "MASSACRE"—JUNE 23, 1925

China in Revolution

An Analysis of Politics and Militarism under the Republic

By

HARLEY FARNSWORTH MACNAIR

HOWARD FERTIG

New York · 1968

HOWARD FERTIG, INC. EDITION 1968
Reissued by arrangement with the University of Chicago Press

Library of Congress Catalog Card Number: 67-24586

PRINTED IN THE UNITED STATES OF AMERICA
BY NOBLE OFFSET PRINTERS, INC.

TO

HENRY MILTON WOLF

IN APPRECIATION OF HIS DISCRIMINATING
INTEREST IN THE FAR EASTERN QUESTION
OVER A PERIOD OF YEARS, THIS STUDY OF
CERTAIN PHASES IS RESPECTFULLY
DEDICATED

PREFACE

DURING the spring of 1930 the writer presented in Chicago a series of public lectures entitled "China in Revolution," under the auspices of the University College of the University of Chicago. Revised and supplemented, these addresses are incorporated in this study of contemporary China. Owing to the limitations of space, and the fact that the foreign relations of this country are considered at length in the writer's collaboration with Dr. H. B. Morse in *Far Eastern International Relations* (Houghton Mifflin), no attempt is made here to discuss the foreign problems involved, except in so far as it has been necessary to refer to them to make clear the domestic situation.

In the lectures an attempt was made, and in this volume it has been continued, to clarify for the non-specialist the conflicting aims, institutions, and personalities involved in a great struggle which has been in process for more than a generation, and which is yet far from completion. The approach is mainly factual, not ideological or idealistic, and is that of the historical student who attempts to be objective and who must be nonpartisan. The patriotic participant in a revolutionary movement may shut his eyes to many disagreeable conditions and assume that, while necessary, they are purely transitory. Those who find their interests adversely affected are likely to assume a condemnatory attitude toward the changes in progress, and may even

attempt to block them by demanding foreign interference on a humanitarian, political, or economic plea.
Whatever the personal feelings of the historian, he must,
if he is to remain true to his profession, disregard them
and present facts and describe conditions as he believes
them to have been.

To do this it has been necessary to list many of the
almost innumerable military campaigns which have
been waged since 1911, and to refer to a great number
of Chinese who have risen above—and, in several
instances, sunk below—the horizon. The harassed and
hasty critic in these United States may be inclined to
cavil at the inclusion of so many wars, and personalities
with (to him) strange-sounding names, and may declare
that he cannot see the forest for the trees. To which it
may be retorted that the author is responsible for
neither, and that the critic is not as greatly incon-
venienced by their numbers as are the people of revolutionary China. To assume that one can comprehend
contemporary conditions in that country without referring to the alarms and tragedies of war, and to the
military and civilian leaders who have played their
complicated rôles therein, is to assume a condition contrary to fact. The reader may skip the names and campaigns if he will, but let him rest assured that having
done so he will remain almost as happily ignorant at the
end as he was at the beginning of his reading. Glib generalizations with vague references to unhappy conditions are easy; the facts are, for the most part, hard, but
the person who wishes to understand modern China may
find them worthy of consideration.

The assembling of material for such a study as this

is a somewhat difficult task—but not for lack of sources and volume. The writer was for considerably more than a decade a resident of China and is enabled, accordingly, to weigh his materials and sift conflicting evidence on the basis of his personal contact with the Chinese and their institutions, and the conditions prevalent in their country. He has made free use of, and gratefully acknowledges his indebtedness to, such sources of information as those contained in *The China Year Book* of the past several years (especially the several excellent chapters on the Kuomingtang by Mr. George E. Sokolsky), Mr. Arnold J. Toynbee's *Survey(s) of International Affairs*, the *Chinese Social and Political Science Review*, the *North China Daily News and Herald*, the *China Weekly Review*, and to personal conferences and correspondence. Particularly valuable for chapter xii were parts of Professor Guy W. Sarvis' diary of his journey up the Yangtze and through Szechwan during the first quarter of 1931, which were placed at the disposal of the author by Mrs. Sarvis.

For reading and criticizing certain chapters of the manuscript the writer wishes to express his thanks to his friends Mr. C. H. Li and Professor Samuel N. Harper, who are not, however, to be assumed as being in accord with the point of view and interpretations of fact presented. To Mr. Clarence Hendershot, also, gratitude is expressed for making available the photograph used as a frontispiece.

The flood of material, critical and uncritical, on contemporary China and its ready accessibility appear to render the inclusion of a bibliography unnecessary.

University of Chicago
June 15, 1931

TABLE OF CONTENTS

TABLE OF CONTENTS

CHAPTER I

THE BACKGROUND

THE revolution through which China is now passing is one which affects all phases of life. There are half-a-dozen or more revolutions in progress: social, political, military, economic, intellectual, religious. It would be difficult to find any aspect of the life of the Chinese people which is not being affected at the present moment. A hasty consideration might lead one to the conclusion that nothing but confusion has thus far resulted from the changes now taking place; at times one is inclined to conclude that the more China changes the more it remains the same. This is owing to the vast size of the country geographically, the huge population, the lack of easy means of communication, and the fact that the culture and civilization of the Chinese people are ancient and largely autochthonous. The question is often asked, "How long will it be before the Chinese will settle down and behave themselves? When will the revolution stop revolving?" To which one generally replies hopefully, "Perhaps in another hundred years."

Fundamentally the revolutionary movements are the result of China's contacts with foreign peoples, ideas, and institutions both at home and abroad; that is to say, the foreign influences so powerful within the past few generations have been in part brought to China by aliens and in part—to a greater degree than is ordinarily credited—by the Chinese people themselves who have gone abroad and returned to their native lands affected by their experiences abroad.

Politically or dynastically speaking, China has undergone many revolutions in the past. The country never has constituted an unchanging entity in a world of change; this is a superficial view which both Chinese and foreigners have fostered, but it is a view contrary to fact as any student of China must admit after even a little study. Another statement which may as well be refuted at the outset is that the Chinese are an essentially pacifistic people as compared with other groups of the human race. The numerous dynastic changes and the civil wars and rebellions from which the country has suffered from the dawn of history, as well as the growth of China territorially into a vast empire, are sufficient to demonstrate the truth of the assertion that the Chinese are no less human, and no more divine, than other peoples when it comes to fighting and acquiring. Unlike their neighbors, the Japanese, the Chinese long ago developed a theory of the mandate of heaven, the voice of the people, and the right to revolt against rulers who are too weak and corrupt to rule them. As long as a dynasty was strong and able to hold by might what it had gained by might, it was clear to the Chinese that that dynasty ruled by the mandate of heaven. When a dynasty grew weak and the people rebelled successfully, it was clear that the mandate of heaven had been exhausted and that heaven willed the rise of a new imperial house. Heaven made its will known through the voice of the people. There might, of course, be a conflict of voices, in which case the will of heaven was made known by the virtue which lies in the sword. Napoleon's dictum with reference to heaven being on the side of the heaviest battalions is not a new thought to the Chinese.

Down to 1911 history may be said, in a sense, to have often repeated itself. Until that date there had never been an essential change in the form of the government of the country—only in the personnel of the dynasty. The overthrow of the Manchus in 1911–12 was complicated, however, by two essentially new factors: first, new ideas of government which led to the attempt to establish a new form of government—a republic instead of a monarchy; and, second, what may, for the sake of brevity, be called "imperialism," that is, the interference of foreign nations with China in order to defend, and perhaps extend, their rights, privileges, and property-holdings in the country. In other words, China had to face at one and the same time complicated domestic and foreign problems, which were affected by new and alien ideas and institutions.

The Manchus who conquered Northern China and founded the Ch'ing dynasty in 1644 had always, but especially from the middle of the nineteenth century, two factors with which to reckon: first, the truth that they themselves were considered by large groups of the Chinese as aliens who should be expelled at the earliest possible opportunity; and, second, the foreign problem, that of dealing with peoples who differed vitally from the Chinese in culture and civilization. The Manchus were ever on the horns of a dilemma: If they followed Chinese thought and method, maintained an attitude of superiority to foreigners and all things foreign, held the foreigners at arm's length, and procrastinated on all occasions of settlements with the foreigners, they encouraged foreign aggression which in turn was bound to expose the essential weakness of the Manchus to the peoples they were ruling. If, on the other hand, the Manchus were friendly to the foreigners, as some of them at times tended to be, and if they attempted to appease the foreigners, they alienated the Chinese and weakened their own position as rulers of the empire. In a very real sense they fell between two stools. Generally speaking, they chose the first method, that of holding the foreigners as far off as possible and claiming complete superiority to everything alien, with the result that there occurred a series of struggles—military and diplomatic—with the Western powers, and finally with Japan, which had in the meantime chosen another solution to practically the same problem.

As the failure of the Manchus to hold the foreigners at bay became evident to the Chinese people, the latter were more than ever encouraged to seek means of expelling their alien rulers. Secret societies, and others not so secret, were formed for the purpose of ousting the Manchus and saving the country by restoring the Chinese themselves to rule. Two out of many rebellions may be mentioned: the Taiping Rebellion, which raged from 1850 to 1864, and the Boxer Rebellion of 1900. The Manchus were compelled at times to lean on the foreigners to control the Chinese; at other times they leaned on the Chinese to control, and attempt to expel, the foreigners. In the case of the Taiping Rebellion the Manchus ultimately received foreign aid; in that of the Boxers they turned a movement which was originally largely anti-Manchu into one which was anti-foreign.

The idea of divide and rule, of playing off one "foreign barbarian" against another, is an age-old one in China. The alternative to this, domestic reform, was never acted upon prior to the close of the Sino-Japanese War of 1894–95, and then very ineffectively.

Before the outbreak of that war in 1894, Sun Yat-sen drew up and presented a memorial to the throne in which he advocated reform. This document was signed by many of the Cantonese gentry. It accomplished nothing at the time. At the close of the war, another Cantonese, Kang Yu-wei, drew up another memorial signed by more than one thousand literati or scholars of many provinces who had taken the second degree— Kujen, approximately equal to the Western A.M. Kang's memorial contained proposals of reform and protested against the ratification of the Treaty of Shimonoseki. This also was without immediate effect. Various reform societies were organized only, for the most part, to be suppressed and driven underground to become secret societies with which China has for centuries been honeycombed.

For many years the seeds of new thought, which were considered to be revolutionary, have been in the process of germination. A Chinese official some years ago remarked that the Chinese revolution really began with the appearance of Robert Morrison in Canton in 1807. Even before the first five treaty ports were opened in 1842 Christian missionaries had been scattering the seeds of new thought among the Chinese of Canton, Macao, and Malaysia and, surreptitiously, even in China proper—for Christianity had never died out in China after its proscription by the Manchu emperor Yung-chêng in 1724. With the opening of the treaty ports following the signing of the Treaty of Nanking in 1842, and with the inclusion of the toleration clauses in later treaties and agreements, Christian missionaries scattered over a large part of China. Their mere presence as physical and intellectual aliens was an incitement to new, and dangerous, thought. Their schools were gradually built up, and these became centers of modern—and, incidentally, Western—learning.

South China was one of the last parts of the empire to come under the control of the Manchus in the seventeenth century. It is far from Peking, and this distance was enhanced in an age without railroads and telegraphs. It was the part always most subject to non-Chinese influence. This has been so from the days of the Roman Empire. From Kwangtung had gone for centuries many thousands of Chinese to Malaysia—the Philippine Islands, Singapore, the East Indies. With the appearance of the modern steamship they went in numbers to Australia, New Zealand, Hawaii, and North and South America. From all these areas many returned to the ancestral homes either to retire on their savings or to visit for a period and dazzle their kinsmen with their new wealth and their foreign ways of life. Whether the returned Chinese stayed in or again left their native land, they brought with them new ideas and ways of conduct which were generally not pleasing to, and not encouraged by, the local officials, either Chinese or Manchu. For the persecution of returned Chinese the Manchus generally received the blame, inasmuch as it was easier and pleasanter to blame the alien ruler than the shortcomings of their own people. The tendency to hold the Manchus responsible for all of China's weaknesses and to believe that the difficulties and drawbacks of living and doing business in China would disappear if they were overthrown was of the greatest possible aid to Sun Yat-sen in the last years of the nineteenth century. Finally, there was Hongkong, after 1842, as a center of modern thought and administration at the very door of Kwangtung. This was an ever present and impregnable criticism of conditions as they were in China. In Kwangtung had been born the leader of the Taiping Rebellion, Hung Siu-ch'üan, and from that province and the neighboring one of Kwangsi had swept the rebels to the Yangtsze Valley in 1852–53.

Taking these facts into consideration, it is not surprising that the two men Sun Yat-sen and Kang Yu-wei who drew up the reform memorials in 1894–95 should have hailed from Kwangtung.

Sun Yat-sen was born on November 12, 1866, in the village of Tsui-heng, a point approximately halfway between Macao and Canton, in the district of Hsiang-shan, Kwangtung province. His parents were peasants of no education, but, according to tradition, the child was from a tender age studious, critical of old methods, and progressive in outlook. At the age of eleven—some say thirteen—years he went to Hawaii, where an older brother had been for some years, and there he received his first impressions of foreign life and institutions. Apparently he lost no time in making comparisons of life in Hawaii with that in China, to the detriment of the latter. He remained in the islands until 1884 when, on

account of fear that the youth was becoming denation-
alized, his brother sent him back to China. His revolutionary ideas along social, political, and religious lines,
and the carrying-out of demonstrations of certain of
them, resulted in his expulsion from Tsui-heng by the
village fathers. After studying for a year in a medical
school in Canton, Sun entered Queen's College in Hongkong. Shortly afterward he embraced Christianity. The
course of the Franco-Chinese War of 1884–85, in the
light of the earlier defeats of China in the years 1839–42
and 1856–60, and his own comparisons of Chinese and
Western methods of life, confirmed him in his anti-
Manchu tendencies.

From 1887 to 1892 Sun Yat-sen studied in the College
of Medicine at Hongkong; in the latter year he became
that institution's first graduate. In the same year he became a member of the Young China party, or association
for the resurrection of China, which had been founded
in 1885. Mainly as a cover for revolutionary propagandizing, in which he had been steadily engaged during his
course of study, he took up the practice of medicine in
Macao and Yangcheng. His chief aids during his ap-
prentice years as a revolutionist were Chen Shao-pai, Yu
Shao-huan, and Yang Hao-ling. The four friends and
conspirators were referred to by their critics as the "four
great pirates" or the "quadrumvirate of great bandits,"
and it was not without difficulty that they gathered
followers.[1]

In 1894 the young doctor established a branch of the

[1] Cf. P. M. d'Elia, "The Life of Dr. Sun Yat-sen," *North China Herald*,
CLXXVII, No. 3299 (October 28, 1930), 137; also F. C. Chen, *La revolution
chinoise* (Paris, 1929), p. 27.

Ko-lao-hwei, or Elder Brother Society, in Canton. This secret, anti-Manchu society dates from at least the middle of the seventeenth century—when the Manchus seized the throne of China—and has played a prominent part in domestic rebellions and antiforeign movements on various occasions. As a member of a deputation to a local official in Canton, Sun narrowly escaped arrest in the same year. In the autumn of the following year, 1895, he was involved in a raid on Canton from Hongkong in co-operation with a revolutionary movement from Swatow. This failed, some seventy of the participants were arrested, and several were executed. Sun himself escaped. Unable to obtain a refuge in either Hongkong or Macao on account of his revolutionary activities, he went to Hawaii, the United States, and England. On this journey he began his organization of overseas revolutionary societies. These were anti-Manchu and pro-republican in their aim. Upon these overseas groups of Chinese, who came largely from Kwangtung, Sun always relied for encouragement and financial aid. The part played by these organizations in the revolutionary movement can scarcely be exaggerated.

A year after his Canton raid Sun was kidnapped in London, in October, 1896, and imprisoned in the Chinese legation. With the aid of a waiter he succeeded in letting Dr. (later Sir) James Cantlie, one of his former instructors in medicine, know of his plight; the latter immediately applied to the British cabinet with the result that Lord Salisbury himself intervened to bring about the prisoner's release. From this time Sun never ceased his preparation for the overthrow of the Manchus and the institution of a republic, but until 1912 he was in the background, with a price upon his head.

Kang Yu-wei, born in 1858, was less radical than Sun Yat-sen. He was given a classical Chinese education and became a brilliant scholar. He did not, however, limit his studies to the Chinese classics. He became especially interested in the reforms of Peter the Great in Russia and in the contemporary reform of Japan, which rose during his lifetime from the position of an insignificant feudal state to that of a world-power.

Strictly speaking, Kang Yu-wei was an evolutionist rather than a revolutionist. Though opposed to the empress dowager, Tzŭ-hsi, he was loyal both to the monarchical form of government and to the Ch'ing dynasty. He was an advocate, however, of a limited constitutional monarchy, or crowned republic, in which the emperor should play a real, though not a dominating, rôle. He also advocated the reform of the old mandarinate. To check the power of the monarch Kang advocated the development of local self-government with gradual participation therein of the people; he also wished the formation of a constitution. In his political philosophy he was distinctly, and remained to the end of his life, a monarchist.

The defeat of China in the war with Japan was followed by the "Battle of Concessions"; these were the immediate causes of a reform movement, membership in which was not limited to Southern Chinese. There was, for example, Chang Chih-tung, a native of the metropolitan province of Chihli. Born in 1835, Chang rose by way of the official literary examinations to high office. From 1884 to 1889 he was Canton viceroy; here he was

undoubtedly influenced by the spirit of change and reform. In 1894 he became Nanking viceroy. The defeat
of China by the Japanese convinced him, as it had Sun
and Kang, of the need for reform, and on the close of
that struggle he collected and published a series of lectures to his subordinates under the title *Exhortations
to Learn.*

The five objects of knowledge as outlined by Viceroy
Chang were:

1. Know the shame of not being like Japan, Turkey, Siam, and
   Cuba.
2. Know the fear that we shall become as India, Annam, Burmah,
   Korea, Egypt, and Poland.
3. Know that if we do not change our customs we cannot reform
   our methods, and if we do not reform our methods we cannot
   utilize the modern implements of war, etc.
4. Know what is important. The study of the old is not urgent; the
   call for men of attainments in useful knowledge is pressing.
   Foreign education is of different kinds. Western handicraft is not
   in demand, but a knowledge of the methods of foreign governments is a consummation devoutly to be wished.
5. Know what is radical. When abroad, do not forget your own
   native country; when you see strange customs, do not forget your
   parents; and let not much wisdom and ingenuity make you forget
   the holy sages.

The "three things necessary to be done in order to
save China from revolution" were declared to be (1) the
maintenance of the reigning dynasty; (2) the conserving
of the holy religion—Confucianism, and (3) the protection of the Chinese race. Chang Chih-tung declared that
a republican form of government was not suited to
China.

The young emperor, Kwang-hsü, was delighted with
the viceroy's work, composed as it was in the purest of
literary Chinese and filled with the spirit of reform. He

ordered its distribution among the governors and viceroys of the empire. More than a million copies are said to have been sold. As a reformer and encourager of modern learning Chang must be counted among those who unwittingly prepared the way for revolution of a kind which he himself abhorred. A revolutionist in the ordinarily accepted sense of the word he assuredly was not. He was a literary aristocrat and a mandarin of the mandarins; with assurance he held that "the fate of China depends upon the literati alone." How far modern China has gone from the way laid down by Chang Chih-tung the events and the conditions of the past decade amply demonstrate. When the hundred days of reform of 1898 were over, and reform was no longer fashionable, Chang scampered back to the ranks of the conservatives, horrified at what he hoped the country might escape, and encouraged the Empress Dowager in her tireless pursuit of those who would muddy the waters of China's crystal stream of culture.

Early in June, 1898, Wêng T'ung-ho, imperial grand tutor, brought to the attention of the Emperor, now in his twenty-sixth year, the name of Kang Yu-wei whose literary works had made him famous. Among these were *The Book of Great Similitudes*, *The Reform of Japan*, and *The Reform of Russia*. Since 1894 the young Emperor had been interested in Western religion and customs; one reason for this had been the presentation to his aunt, the Empress Dowager, of a finely bound copy of the New Testament by more than ten thousand Chinese Christian women on the occasion of Tzŭ-hsi's sixtieth birthday anniversary. Kwang-hsü now became acquainted with Kang Yu-wei's works dealing with the reforms of Peter the Great and those which had contributed to the rise of Japan. Greatly impressed, he appointed Kang to official position and honored him with a personal audience on June 14, 1898. Now began the so-called "hundred days of reform" during which scores of edicts were issued by the Emperor at the behest of the enthusiast, Kang. Among these may be mentioned such outstanding ones as the following:

JUNE 23.—Abolishing the Wenchang essay as a prominent feature in the examinations leading to official office

JULY 10.—Establishing schools and colleges in all district cities and ordering that all memorial and unofficial temples should be used for the purpose

AUG. 10.—Ordering the Tientsin and Nanking viceroys to consult and report on the establishment of a naval academy and training ships

AUG. 30.—Abolishing many minor and sinecurist positions in Peking and the provinces

SEPT. 5.—Foreshadowing a national army, based on conscription, to be drilled according to Western method.

SEPT. 16.—Sanctioning a system of annual, published budgets.

These and other edicts struck at the roots of corruption, inefficiency, and general conservatism throughout the empire and, of course, brought the imperial reformer and his philosophical adviser into conflict, direct and indirect, with innumerable vested interests.

Second only to Kang Yu-wei among the reformers in Peking at this time was T'an Tzu-t'ung, another Cantonese, a son of the governor of Hupeh, and, in 1898, one of the secretaries of the Grand Council. T'an was a philosopher of energy and positive action; he differed with Kang Yu-wei in the radicalism of his thought and his willingness to die in defense of his ideals. He is reported by Liang Ch'i-ch'ao to have remarked:

"The. weakness of China is due to the fact that there have been no martyrs for the cause of freedom and reform. Shall I not be the first martyr?" Again he said, "Blood must flow before things can be better." T'an was an anti-authoritarian opposed to the classical thinkers of China, especially Lao-tsze. To the latter he attributed the weakness of the Chinese people in their negative and passive attitude toward life. An unbeliever in non-resistance, quietism, renunciation, and absolutism, he held that the ancient teachings with reference to universal obligation between the ruler and his subjects had been corrupted. He ardently advocated the rights of the people, particularly that of revolution.

Unlike Kang, T'an was a revolutionist rather than an evolutionist; like Sun Yat-sen, T'an worked for the overthrow of the Manchus whom he considered hopelessly corrupt. Among the papers of Kang Yu-wei later found at his birthplace in Kwangtung was one in which T'an was advocated as worthy to be nominated to the office of president of the Chinese Republic. T'an was the most distinguished radical official of the period.

Of the Cantonese reformers the most distinguished scholar was Liang Ch'i-ch'ao, the editor of a reforming organ in Peking called *Chinese Progress*. Liang, like Kang, was a sincere believer in constitutional monarchy. He was not a revolutionist; clear proof of this is to be found in his message to Yuan Shih-kai in 1915 when the latter was engaged in his monarchical scheme. Liang wrote: ". . . . A change in the conduct of a government is a sign of progress, while a change in the form of a government is a sign of revolution. A revolution always retards the progress of a nation." Among the edicts issued by the Emperor during the hundred days was that of August 16, ordering the establishment of a Government Bureau of Translation. Over this Liang was appointed to preside; standard works on political economy and natural science were to be translated and published. He was granted the sum of one thousand taels a month to cover the expenses involved in his work. Liang was not so much an original thinker as an eloquent channel for the expression of new thought. In this period he advocated material improvements and the reorganization of education but said little, however much he may have thought, concerning democracy and popular sovereignty.

Watchfully waiting in the "profound" seclusion of her palace during the summer of 1898 was the old empress dowager, Tzŭ-hsi, who had forced the election of her nephew to the throne on the death of her son in 1875. The first two or three of the reform decrees had at least her formal approval. As the progress of the sun chariot became more and more irregular, however, and gave evidence of leaving the old established course entirely, she began to take measures to change drivers.

The liberalism of the reformers toward the end of August, and during the first days of September, 1898, led to protests on the part of the conservatives in office, and they begged the Empress Dowager to resume her rule. Kang Yu-wei now advised the Emperor to strengthen his position by seizing and imprisoning the Dowager who, he was convinced, was a source of danger to reform. Into the details of the ensuing plots and counterplots it is not necessary to enter;[1] suffice to say

[1] Cf. J. O. P. Bland and E. T. Backhouse, *China under the Empress Dowager*, chap. xii; E. T. Williams, *China Yesterday and Today* (4th ed.), pp. 493–96; H. B. Morse, *The International Relations of the Chinese Empire*, III, 141–46; B. L. Putnam-Weale, *The Fight for the Republic in China*, pp. 26–28.

that the plan of the reformers to imprison Tzǔ-hsi failed, and the Emperor himself became a state prisoner. Kang and Liang fled the country; T'an Tzu-t'ung refused to flee and, with several other reformers, was beheaded in the public market place of Peking. The Empress Dowager and her conservative followers entered upon an antireform campaign. An offer of one hundred thousand taels was made for the capture of Kang Yuwei dead or alive. His writings were ordered destroyed, likewise the graves of his ancestors, and an attempt was made to put to death all his kinsmen. The reform decrees of the summer of 1898 were reversed; the magazine *Chinese Progress* was suppressed, and an attempt was made to forget, temporarily, that the condition of the empire left anything to be desired.

Followed now, upon the failure of both reformers and revolutionists, and as a result of the scramble for concessions of the years 1897–99, the Boxer Rebellion. This movement was originally in part directed against the Manchus. The court was shrewd and strong enough to turn it into an antiforeign outbreak. As a result Peking fell into the hands of the allied armies in 1900, the court fleeing to Sian-fu in Shensi.

The failure of China's rulers to kill or expel all foreigners encouraged the reformers and revolutionists to renewed endeavors. Returning from Shensi to her polluted palaces in the capital, the Empress Dowager at last realized that reform only, or at least the pretense of reform, could prevent a revolution which must overthrow the dynasty. Accordingly, she set out on the road earlier traveled by the young Emperor, and edicts were published which, in several cases, were similar to those

issued in 1898, and which had resulted in the imprisonment of Kwang-hsü.

The next decade witnessed a government-fostered attempt to stem radicalism, by the projected assimilation
of the Manchus with the Chinese, and by the gradual
bringing-in of a constitutional régime which should
introduce representative institutions and result in a
limited monarchy not greatly different from that advocated by Kang Yu-wei, but falling far short of the aims
of either Sun Yat-sen or T'an Tzu-t'ung.

The results of two earlier educational movements—
that of the Christian missionaries and the Yung Wing
educational mission of 1872–81—were becoming increasingly evident. Chinese who had enjoyed the advantages of a modern education, either abroad or in their
homeland, and who had for long been kept in the background now began to rise to power. Government-
fostered colleges and universities along modern lines
were opened. In 1903 a ministry of education was established. Two years later the old classical examination
system, which is to be traced back at least as far as the
T'ang dynasty, was abolished by a stroke of the ver-
milion pencil. This constituted a break with China's
intellectual past none the less violent in that it took
place by imperial decree.

In September, 1906, an imperial edict promised administrative reform along legal, financial, naval, and
military lines. It was now declared that the nation
should be prepared for the gradual introduction of a
constitutional government. Another decree, issued on
November 6, announced the abolition of the old ministries and the substitution for them of thirteen new

ministries; also a national consultative assembly of elected representatives was provided for. In the following year this assembly was ordered placed on a working basis, and provincial consultative assemblies were also created. On Christmas Day, 1907, an imperial decree promised an elected Parliament with powers to enact laws and control the executive. On the following August 27 (1908) a nine years' program of reform was outlined, at the end of which period Parliament should be summoned to function. A draft constitution was published at the same time. The first article of this declared that "the Ta Tsing dynasty shall rule over the Ta Tsing Empire forever, and shall be honored through all the ages"—an optimistic declaration indicating that the Manchus and their advisers had been studying the constitution of Japan.

For the second time an effort was being made to reform China from the top, and the second essay was to prove no more successful than that of a decade earlier. No attempt was made to go to the root of China's governmental troubles, financial and judicial, to bring in a system of salaries for officials and require them to relinquish to the central government the sums collected by them. The old system of perquisites remained intact, and the imperial government continued to suffer financially. No effort was put forth to remedy judicial weakness and institute a judiciary manned by trained officials. The idea of a Parliament was entirely alien; moreover, few Chinese were qualified for membership in such an institution. This was to be abundantly demonstrated within a few years. Had there been no foreign problem, or had there been an able native ruler with competent advisers to oversee and guide the developments outlined, the country might have avoided a violent revolution as had Japan. Neither of these conditions held; the interests and jealousies of the powers were intertwined with domestic problems, while the government was still controlled by the extreme conservatives, a majority of the high officeholders being Manchus who were more interested in holding what they had than in bringing about reform.

On November 14, 1908, the deposed emperor, Kwang-hsü, ascended the dragon chariot to visit his ancestors on high, to be followed the next day by the Empress Dowager—who was less interested, perhaps, in overseeing his actions in the next life than in preventing his return to power without her tutelage on the earthly plane. The throne was passed on to a three-year-old nephew of Kwang-hsü who was given the reign-title of Hsüan T'ung. Prince Ch'un, the father of the Emperor, was appointed regent. Throughout the provinces the Chinese pressed for a rapid continuation of reform, or plotted the overthrow of the Manchus with the object of bringing in a native dynasty, or establishing a republic.

In October, 1909, the provincial assemblies met. In reality they were merely debating societies, but they proceded to demand that the convening of the promised national Parliament should be pushed forward so that it should meet within two years. This the imperial government refused in January of the following year. In October of that year, 1910, the first national assembly was convened in Peking under the presidency of an imperial prince. After some hesitation the government issued a decree summoning Parliament for the year 1913. The national assembly was not satisfied and insisted on an immediate summons for Parliament; moreover, the demand was made that the Grand Council should become responsible to Parliament. The imperial government promised to consider the matter and, on January 11, 1911, the assembly was prorogued.

On May 8, 1911, further changes were made in the imperial government in a vain attempt to meet the demands of the reformers. Three of the old higher councils of state were abolished; in their place a cabinet and a Privy Council were created. Prince Ch'ing, an aged Manchu, corrupt and of mediocre ability, who had served as president of the abolished Grand Council, was appointed prime minister. This gave evidence that the Manchus were unwilling to grant real reform; a change in administrative forms, without change of personnel, meant little to those who were seeking a relocation of authority.

Concurrently with the weakening of the imperial government, and with the growing demand for reform, there developed a provincial autonomy movement in the western and central provinces of China. This in itself was not so much a new development as a revivification of an old principle. Rarely has China had anything approaching a truly centralized government. The people and the local officials have always opposed such. This was a fact that westerners and their governments were exceedingly slow to appreciate in the nineteenth century. In general, the West pictured old China as an absolute monarchy; it held that all that was necessary was to bring pressure to bear on the imperial government in order to get what it wanted. This accounts largely for the determination of the British government in 1858 and 1860 to obtain the right of residence at Peking for its envoy—a right which the other powers insisted upon as soon as England had won it. This insistence and pressure constituted one of the manifold factors which weakened the imperial government of the Manchus and encouraged the Chinese to seek its overthrow. Under the pseudo-republic since 1912 the old problem of a loose versus a centralized government has persisted as one of the great problems which is as yet unsolved and which probably will so continue for many years to come. It constituted an immediate cause for the outbreak of the revolution of 1911.

CHAPTER II

YUAN SHIH-KAI *vs.* SUN YAT-SEN—THE
FIRST PHASE

THE period 1912–16 was one which witnessed a struggle in China between two outstanding characters, Sun Yat-sen and Yuan Shih-kai, their followers, and the ideas which motivated them. Sun and Yuan were intellectually antipodal. Sun was a southerner; Yuan was a northerner. Sun was a radical revolutionist demanding the overthrow of the Manchus and the establishment of a republican form of government. Yuan was moderately liberal, an exponent of the old mandarinate of the empire, and a believer in monarchical institutions. Prior to 1912 Sun held no public office. Yuan, on the contrary, rose through the civil service to become by force of circumstance a military leader. Though the father of the modern war lords of China, Yuan was not, contrary to popular supposition, a professional militarist but a civilian official.

Yuan Shih-kai was born in an official family in the north-central province of Honan in 1860. He was, accordingly, six years older than his great antagonist, Sun. As a protégé of Li Hung-chang, Yuan was sent to Korea in 1884 as Chinese resident. There he remained, in Seoul, the capital, for a decade, distinguishing himself by his boldness and energy in opposing the Japanese and attempting to maintain the *status quo* of Korea as a vassal state to China. The hatred for Yuan engendered

in the minds of the Japanese during this period was to
have a profound effect upon his later career. Returning
to his homeland, Yuan was appointed, in 1895, to the
position of civil commandant of a division of five thousand foreign-drilled troops of the Peiyang or northern
army. Not long after he was made provincial judge of
Chihli. His superior in command of the army was Jung
Lu, a Manchu, who was viceroy of Chihli and a close
friend and supporter of the old Empress Dowager. With
Jung Lu, Yuan participated in a ceremony by which the
two men became what the Chinese call "blood brothers,"
that is, supporters of each other to death. When the
hundred days of reform of 1898 were drawing to a close,
and the emperor, Kwang-hsü, was planning to compass
the seizure and imprisonment of Tzǔ Hsi, Yuan was
called to Peking by the Emperor, who planned to place
him in command of the army and with it complete his
schemes. It is scarcely necessary to remark that the
Emperor knew nothing of the blood brotherhood of
Yuan and Jung Lu. By two decrees Yuan was breveted
vice-president of a ministry, appointed viceroy ad interim of Chihli, and made commander of the Peiyang
army. How precise were the directions of the Emperor
to Yuan will probably never be known, and upon
them rests the technical decision as to whether Yuan
actually betrayed the Emperor. The consensus of opinion has always been that he did, although, naturally,
Yuan denied this. In any case, the plot to imprison the
Empress failed and the first chapter in the revolution
was ended.

During the last period of the Empress Dowager's rule
Yuan was in favor at court and the holder of high office.

In December, 1899, he became acting governor of Shantung; in the following March he became substantive
governor of that province. Throughout the Boxer outbreak he maintained order within his jurisdiction, a fact
which strengthened his relations with the powers in later
years. On the death of Li Hung-chang in November,
1901, Yuan was at once appointed to succeed him as
viceroy of the metropolitan province of Chihli. During
the second period of reform, that is, the constitutional
movement under Manchu direction, following the Boxer
settlement, Yuan was one of the most powerful supporters of gradual modernization.

Although on the death of the Empress Dowager in
mid-November, 1908, Yuan was appointed to still higher
court rank, he fell from power six weeks later, being
ordered on January 2, 1909, to resign his offices and retire to his home in Honan. His fall was probably due to
the fear engendered in the Manchus by his control of
the most powerful military force in the north as much
as to the treacherous rôle he was supposed to have
played in 1898.

For two and a half years Yuan was in retirement.
Then, on the outbreak of the Wuchang revolution, he
was recalled by the Manchus. After some hesitation he
accepted appointment as Wuchang viceroy; shortly afterward he became commander-in-chief of the imperial
forces. So much, then, for the background of Yuan Shih-
kai, the Chinese arch-opponent of Sun Yat-sen until the
summer of 1916.

The career of Sun Yat-sen, the most influential of
China's revolutionists in modern times, may now be
traced. In no wise daunted by his narrow escape from

death in 1896, Sun remained for about two years, 1896–98, in Europe studying the political, social, and economic conditions of that continent, and planning methods for a complete revolution in his own country which should once for all save the Chinese from their own weaknesses and from foreign aggression. This period witnessed the germination of the ideas of Sun which came later to be known as the "three people's principles." These, it has been said, were suggested by Lincoln's phrase, "government of the people, by the people, and for the people." Since at this time there were few or no Chinese students in Europe among whom Sun could propagandize, he decided, in 1899, to return to Japan where large numbers of young men had gone to study at the close of the Sino-Japanese War.

To Japan, Liang Chi'i-ch'ao had retired shortly after his escape in 1898, while Kang Yu-wei had taken refuge in Malaysia. In these areas Liang and Kang continued to disseminate their theories, which were opposed to the republican ideas of Sun. Owing to this and to the failures of both types of reformers in North and South China, Sun found it no easy task to carry on his propaganda in the period before the Boxer outbreak. He sent his close friend, Chen Shao-pai, to establish a propaganda journal in Hongkong, however, and, contemporaneously, another of his friends, Che Kien-jou, began the task of uniting the secret societies in the Yangtze Valley with those of Kwangtung, Kwangsi, and Fukien. They were united with the Young China party, branches of which Sun had established in Hawaii and the United States after his flight from China in 1895. Thus the secret antidynastic societies of China were brought into touch with similar organizations among the Chinese abroad. The originator of this statesman-like idea is said to have been not Sun but his American friend, Homer Lea. Whether this is correct or not, it was a masterly stroke in building up a well-financed movement against the Manchu government in China.

The Boxer period was seized upon by Sun to make another attempt to start a revolution in South China, at Waichow and Canton. To these cities he dispatched agents and attempted himself to return to China. The English in Hongkong and the Japanese in Formosa prevented his disembarkation in their territories. His revolutionary scheme failed at this time and his friend, Che Kien-jou, who had carried out the unification of the secret societies, was killed. Nevertheless Sun's stock as a patriotic revolutionist went up considerably.

Most of the years 1899–1903 were spent by Sun in Japan. In 1904 he started on another trip around the world, his object being to keep the revolutionary fires burning among the Chinese in foreign lands. Arriving in Europe in the spring of 1905, he met groups of Chinese students in Brussels, Berlin, and Paris, preached to them his "three people's principles" and outlined his constitution of the five powers for a republic.

As early, apparently, as the autumn of 1905 the Tung Men Hwei (union devoted to revolution) was established in Tokyo by the union of the Young China party and other revolutionary societies. Among the conspirators of this period were Huang Shing—a Hunanese, Hu Han-min and Wang Ching-wei—Cantonese, and C. T. Wang—a Chekiangese. This revolutionary society quickly spread to China where it was joined by thousands of young men devoted to reform by any method either peaceful or forcible. In Japan a paper called *Min Pao* (The People) was founded by Hu Han-min and Wang Ching-wei for the purpose of spreading the doctrines of Sun Yat-sen.

As a result of protests on the part of the Manchu imperial government Sun was expelled from Japan by the government in 1906. He went to Indo-China to work among the Chinese in that area; again expelled, he passed on to Malaysia and then to the United States, having left the direction of the movement in the Far East to Huang Hsing and Hu Han-min.

In 1909 occurred the attempted assassination by Wang Ching-wei in Peking of Prince Ch'un, the prince regent, father of the child-emperor. Wang was arrested and condemned to death, but on account of the pressure of public opinion, which the Manchus feared more and more, the sentence of death was commuted to life-imprisonment. On the outbreak of the revolution in 1911 Wang was released.

In 1910 a revolutionary outbreak in Canton was put down. On learning of this revolutionary attempt Sun returned from the United States to Japan where the Japanese officials refused him permission to land; accordingly he journeyed on to Penang, off the west coast of the Malay Peninsula. Money was needed and Sun set about its collection. The authorities of the Dutch East Indies, the English colonies in the East, and of Siam, in turn, refused him permission to reside in their possessions. He therefore returned to America and Europe to propagandize and to collect funds, both of which he did with success, despite the fact that his cause suffered nine

defeats within the space of fifteen years. The last of
Sun's failures before the successful outbreak at Wuchang
in October, 1911, occurred at Canton in April of that
year under the leadership of Huang Hsing. In this attack the Tatar general in command of Manchu troops
at Canton was assassinated, and the vice-regal *yamen*
was burned; but the revolt failed. In it seventy-two
revolutionists lost their lives. Their bodies were interred
at Hoang Hoa Kang, near Canton, and they became
famous as the "seventy-two heroes of Hoang Hoa Kang."

Mention has been made of the growth of a provincial
autonomy movement. The immediate point at issue
was one having to do with railroad construction from
Hankow into Szechwan, and Hankow to Canton.
Stated briefly, the principle at stake was the construction and control of railroads by the provinces themselves versus that of construction and control by the
imperial government. The provinces were jealous of the
increased power which would accrue to the central
government by the control of the railroads; moreover,
they feared that the floating of loans for the purpose
would result in the practical, if not theoretical, loss of
Chinese sovereignty in China proper as had, to a great
degree, been the case in Manchuria.

The director-in-chief of railway construction was a
corrupt and unpopular official, Sheng Hsüan-hwei
(Kung-pao), who had been appointed to office in 1896.
His policy was one of centralization of governmental
control. In January, 1911, he became president of the
ministry of communications. On May 20 a contract for
large railway loans was signed by Sheng and the representatives of a four-power group representing England,

France, Germany, and the United States. In the same month an imperial edict announced the taking-over by the central government of all privately financed railway lines, and the construction and control henceforward of all trunk lines by the central government. There shortly developed a dispute over the settlement with the provinces on the matter of loans and subscriptions already made locally for the building of the proposed lines southward and westward.

It will be noted that this railroad dispute between the central and westward provinces with Peking coincided with the outbreak of the revolutionists in Kwangtung. Unlike the latter, it was not easily put down. Szechwan, in particular, was wrought up over the railway problem, and especially over differences between the central government and those who had subscribed locally for the building of railroads and who demanded the return of their moneys. On August 24, a passive resistance movement, in the form of a strike, began in Chengtu where government students refused to attend classes. In the following month rioting and street-fighting occurred.

The imperial government hesitated. Before its orders could be carried out a bomb exploded in a house in the Russian concession in Hankow on October 9. When the Russian police investigated, they found the place to be headquarters for revolutionists, and plans for the seizure of Wuchang during the following spring, as well as lists of revolutionists, were uncovered. Executions followed, and the leaders, finding their hands forced, decided on immediate revolt. They forced Colonel Li Yuan-hung, a military aid to the viceroy, to lead them, and the revolt began on October 10. Fighting in the

Wuhan area, in which Huang Hsing took a leading
part, lasted for several weeks; this was accompanied by
the rising of revolutionists in various centers, noticeably
in the central and southern provinces. There was considerable bloodshed in Wuhan (Hankow, Hanyang, and
Wuchang), Nanking, and Sian in Shensi, but, compara-
tively speaking, the revolution was a bloodless one.

Of the generals on the Manchu side there was but one
whose loyalty was undoubted and conspicuous. This
was Chang Hsun, who was reputed to have acted as
cart-driver for the Empress Dowager on her trip to
Sian in 1900, when she fled on the fall of Peking to the
allied forces. In Nanking, Chang Hsun demonstrated
his loyalty by taking many heads, particularly those of
students. Ultimately he was forced to retire northward
—where he lived to fight again a losing battle for the
Manchus in 1917.

At the time the revolution broke out in the Wuhan
area, Sun Yat-sen was in the United States. Although
reported to have been anxious to return at once to China
to participate in the movement, he stayed in the West
for a time, engaged in arousing the sympathies of the
United States and Europe on behalf of the revolutionists. From America he went to England and France.
His absence abroad served to keep him out of the maelstrom of conflicting groups and policies of the revolutionists in China. In the meantime the mouthpiece of
the revolutionists became the well-known Wu Ting-fang,
former Chinese minister to the United States.

Early in December a truce was reached between the
Manchus and the revolutionists. In Nanking, the first
capital of the Ming dynasty, an assembly of representa-

tives began to gather from the revolting provinces. Colonel Li Yuan-hung and his colleagues in Central China showed no ability, or desire, to dispute with the diplomatic mouthpiece of revolution in Nanking and Shanghai, and Wu Ting-fang had things rather much his own way.

In Peking the imperial court was making every concession in a vain attempt to save the dynasty. As his representative, Yuan Shih-kai sent T'ang Shao-yi, an American-educated Cantonese, to confer with Wu Ting-fang and his henchmen. T'ang reached Shanghai on December 17, and within a few days allowed himself to be converted to republicanism. Whether T'ang betrayed Yuan, or was acting in collusion with him in choosing this method of deserting the Manchus, is a moot point. Yuan's own remarks to Morrison, the distinguished correspondent in Peking of the *London Times*, as well as his later actions, indicate clearly that he had no admiration or desire for a republican form of government in China. Said he: "The institution of a republic could only mean the instability of a rampant democracy, of dissension and partition, amid which all interests would suffer and for several decades there would be no peace in the empire." Li Yuan-hung had already intimated to Yuan his belief that the latter was working for his own interests when he aided the Manchus. It is more than possible that Yuan was willing that T'ang should be converted to republicanism as a diplomatic means of ridding China of the Manchus and of preparing the way to the throne for himself.

In any case it was apparent that Yuan could not conquer Central and Southern China for the Manchus who were practically bankrupt owing to Sun Yat-sen's successful persuasion of the British government not to lend money to the imperial government at this time. Nor could the revolutionists oust Yuan from the north where he was securely intrenched. For better or for worse each must accept the other for the time being. From Europe, Sun reached Shanghai on December 24, 1911. Three days later the Nanking Provisional Assembly went to Shanghai to beg him to accept the presidency of the provisional government of the united provinces of China. To this the distinguished revolutionist agreed. On the twenty-ninth the election was held in Nanking, and on January 1, 1912, the indomitable antagonist of the Manchus assumed office. Shortly afterward in solemn state he appeared before the tomb of Hung Wu, the founder of the last native dynasty—the Ming—which had ruled China. To the spirit of the man who had ousted the Mongols, Sun announced the expulsion of the alien Manchus.

In his cabinet the provisional president included Huang Hsing as minister of war, and Wu Ting-fang as minister of justice. To heal the breach between north and south Sun offered to resign in favor of Yuan Shih-kai, who should remain as provisional president until a permanent government could be formed. Although the latter at first declined, this was the solution later agreed upon. After six and half weeks' tenure of office Dr. Sun retired in favor of Yuan.

On February 12, the boy-emperor, Hsuan T'ung, abdicated, generous terms of provision for the imperial family having been submitted, and the court retired for the time being to Jehol in Tartary beyond the Great Wall. Three days later Yuan was elected provisional president, having been won over, in the meantime, to vocal approval of republicanism. Thus the third phase in the history of China's revolution was completed.

CHAPTER III

YUAN SHIH-KAI *vs.* SUN YAT-SEN—
THE SECOND PHASE

INSTEAD of healing the breach between the north and the south, the retirement of Dr. Sun and the election of Yuan resulted in making it wider and clearer. Sun's followers disagreed with Yuan, and what he stood for, on almost every point. They desired a popular, democratic republic in reality, based on a wide franchise, and a powerful legislature which should dictate to the executive. They wanted change overnight. They expected Yuan to be their willing tool, and to retire as soon as a permanent government should be formed.

Yuan needed southern revolutionary support, and intended to use the revolutionists in bringing the country under his control. He had no intention of hastily attempting to bring the people into a participation in the central government for which nothing in their background had prepared them. Moreover, he had no intention of accepting dictation from anyone—least of all from a popularly elected legislature controlled by southerners. As events proved, he had no intention of retiring from the executive position; on the contrary, there is reason to believe that he planned a return to monarchy from the beginning. Above all, he was not interested in socialism, state or otherwise, and this Sun and most of his followers were working for. Yuan was willing to bring in gradual reform in line with the experience of

34

the Chinese people; he was unalterably opposed to deep-rooted revolution and a complete break with the past. Provincialism was much stronger than nationalism, and, as previously stated, Yuan was a northerner with little love for the southerners, or for the ideas of overseas Chinese who had been so lacking in a sense of propriety as to leave their homeland and ancestral tombs to reside, and to seek a living permanently, among "barbarians."

The provisional president-designate took the oath of office on March 10, 1912; the promulgation of the provisional constitution, the work of the Nanking representatives of the revolution, occurred at the same time. This instrument of government provided for a president, a vice-president, a National Advisory Council, and a Bicameral Assembly. The power was centered in the legislative, instead of the executive, branch. On April 29 the National Advisory Council met. It quickly became evident, by the obstructionist tactics employed, that Sun Yat-sen's supporters were in a majority. Owing largely to these tactics, Parliament was not convened until April of the following year—1913.

In the interval the relations between Yuan and the Kuomingtang, or National People's party, as the revolutionary party of Sun was now called, became more and more strained. To Yuan's aid came a group in opposition to the Kuomingtang known first as the Kunghotang and later as the Chinputang. This party stood for a strong executive; to it belonged Liang Ch'i-ch'ao, Li Yuan-hung, and—more or less uncertainly—Wu Ting-fang.

Yuan's needs for foreign loans, and his desire to supplant by his own men the revolutionary leaders of the provinces, together with his evident disapproval of responsible party government, brought him into conflict with the southerners.

The provisional constitution provided that the permanent constitution should be drafted by a committee of parliament. In opposition to this several of Yuan's followers memorialized him in favor of a permanent constitution to be drafted by a committee appointed by Yuan himself.

In July, 1912, Sung Chiao-jen, a leader of the Kuomintang who was candidate for the office of premier, criticized Yuan for his failure to institute party government. In the following March Sung was assassinated in Shanghai as he was about to board a train to go to Peking for the opening of Parliament and the presumed assumption of the premiership. In the preceding August, General Chang Cheng-wu, a friend of Sun, and a revolutionary leader, had been arrested in Peking and shot without a trial. Sun himself, who was now devoting his attention to the economic development of the country, was invited to Peking where he was appointed director-general of railroads.

When Parliament convened on April 8, 1913, a little over a fortnight after the assassination of Sung, the relations between the newly gathered parliamentarians and the president were so strained that Yuan himself did not appear, nor would the two houses allow his secretary to read his congratulatory message, although they formally received it. Before the two houses could settle their own difficulties and organize for business, they entered upon a struggle with the provisional president over the negotiations with foreign bankers for a loan to the new government. They resented both the requirements of the foreign bankers and the inevitable strengthening of the president's position in a military way.

Yuan and the foreign bankers went ahead with their negotiations despite the protests of the parliamentarians led largely by C. T. Wang, vice-president of the Senate. In May a "reorganization loan" of twenty-five million pounds sterling was floated in London, Paris, Berlin, St. Petersburg, Brussels, and Tokyo. Yuan's position was greatly strengthened, and that of Parliament correspondingly weakened, to the considerable discomfiture of Sun and the southerners. In July, following attempts of Yuan to unseat provincial revolutionary governors and put in their places his own military leaders, the so-called "second revolution" broke out in the Yangtze Valley. Sun Yat-sen and Huang Hsing felt that the provisional president must be chastised, and believed that the country would aid them to do it. Neither the country generally nor the foreigners gave them support or encouragement, and the punitive expedition was a total failure. Many of the parliamentarians fled from Peking, while Sun and Huang, now avowed enemies of Yuan, took refuge in Japan. The Kuomingtang as a whole was not declared to be implicated; this left enough of the parliamentarians to go ahead with the elections which had been postponed on account of the summer revolt.

In October, Yuan was duly elected substantive president of China. To make certain of an election, he had taken the precaution of guarding the entrances and exits lest the parliamentarians leave before agreeing by majority on a candidate. General Li Yuan-hung, who had

held the Wuhan area for Yuan during the summer revolt, was elected vice-president. On October 10, two
years after the Wuchang outbreak of 1911, Yuan was
formally inaugurated in Peking as president of China.

Having put down the revolt of Sun, been formally
elected as president, supplied with funds, and recognized
by the powers, Yuan was ready to proceed to the further
strengthening of his position as personal ruler of the
country. Opportunity presented itself with the final reports of the parliamentary constitutional committee.
The constitution prepared by this group, during the previous four months, was calculated to clip the presidential
claws and wings. The chief executive was to preside
over a cabinet which should be entirely responsible to
Parliament. Without the consent of the premier the
president could do nothing. Such a provision might suit
a French president but never Yuan Shih-kai. Backed by
his military governors, the president prevented the ratification of the new constitution by expelling from Parliament on November 4 all members of the Kuomingtang
on the charge of complicity in the events of the preceding summer. Parliament now was left without a quorum. In December that body was suspended; on January 10, 1914, it was dissolved.

As a concession to appearances Yuan had a new constitution prepared by his supporters and, on May 1
(1914), the "constitutional compact," as it was called,
was promulgated. This basic law made the president
the source of power and lengthened his term of office
from five years—for which he had been elected—to ten
years, and provided for indefinite re-elections. In reality, constitutional government under Yuan was a thin

veil for life-dictatorship of a ruler who depended on military force rather than on the conflicting voices of the people. Yuan was far more powerful than the emperor he had unseated.

The course of the Chinese revolution in 1914 and the following years was affected by developments outside China as had been the case in its earlier phases. Had this not been so it is probable that Yuan might have been successful in his plans to enthrone himself as the founder of a new dynasty. Within three months from the date of the promulgation of the constitutional compact the World War had begun in Europe. Japan now had a better opportunity than hitherto to interfere in Chinese affairs. In December, 1911, she had negotiated with the weakening Manchus and with the Chinese revolutionists. Evidence was not wanting of her plan to intervene in China "for the sake of the peace of the Far East." On December 23, 1911, the Japanese minister to Peking formally announced to Yuan that under no condition would Japan recognize a Chinese republic. Japan's actions resulted in protests from her ally, England, and she modified her tone for a time. When the second revolution broke out, in 1913, the southerners were aided by the Japanese.

The outbreak of war in Europe was followed by an Anglo-Japanese siege of the German-leased territory of Kiaochow in Shantung with accompanying disregard of China's neutrality—which, since it took place in China, was apparently not considered as serious a breach of international law as was the German disregard of the neutrality of Belgium. When the Japanese disregarded China's protest over the breach of her neutrality, Yuan's

government delimited a war zone which the Japanese
disregarded. When, after the fall of Tsingtao and the
taking-over of Germany's interests in Shantung by Japan, China announced the abolition of the war zone on
January 7, 1915, the Japanese minister, Mr. Hioki,
seized the opportunity to present directly to President
Yuan, on January 18, a list of twenty-one demands
which he had been holding since the preceding December 3, awaiting a favorable opportunity to present them.
Had these been accepted by China in their entirety the
country would quickly have been transformed into a
Japanese protectorate.

Far from discouraging Yuan in his plan to make himself emperor, the twenty-one demands served rather as
an impetus. Shortly after the presentation of the Japanese ultimatum of May, 1915, a society for the preser-
vation of peace, the Chou An Hwei, was formed. The
chief object of this organization was the setting-forth of
the desirability of the monarchical system of government for China. Liang Ch'i-ch'ao, Yuan's minister of
justice, refused his support, stating his opposition to a
change in the form of government in the words earlier
quoted. So the dictator fell back on one of Kang Yu-
wei's and Liang Ch'i-ch'ao's followers, a certain Yang
Tu. The latter published a pamphlet in the summer of
1915 arguing that "the country cannot be saved except
through the establishment of a constitutional form of
government. No constitutional form of government can
be formed except through the establishment of a monarchy. The constitutional form of government has a set
of fixed laws, and the monarchy has a definite head who
cannot be changed, in which matters lies the source of
national strength and wealth."

Yuan's constitutional adviser at this time was Dr. Frank J. Goodnow, later president of Johns Hopkins University. The latter now presented a memorandum which declared that the ideal form of government for a state depends rather upon the basic conditions of the country than upon the wishes of the people. With various qualifications and conditions this document contained the statement " .... The monarchical system is better suited to China than the republican system." The words of so able an adviser strengthened the monarchical movement.

Yuan professed to believe the proposed change was "unsuitable to the circumstances of the country," but, acting perhaps on the theory that the right hand should not know what the left hand does, the president-dictator allowed the movement to gather force both in Peking and in the provinces, in spite of the fact that many of his friends deserted him and representatives of Japan, Great Britain, and Russia advised delay. The monarchical machinery erected in the provinces worked smoothly and, during the autumn of 1915, the "elections" of Yuan to the throne were carried out with a remarkable show of unanimity. In fact, there was too high a degree of harmony; it was unnatural in China. After the counting of the ballots in December, the council of state formally invited Yuan to "obey the true will of the people and ascend the throne." Like Caesar, Yuan thrice declined the crown. He finally capitulated, however, all the dictates of custom and good taste under such circumstances having been carried out, and he announced his enthronement for January 1, 1916, choosing for his reign-title the characters Hung Hsien ("glorious constitutionalism").

In the meantime, what of Dr. Sun? As mentioned above, he had again taken refuge in Japan, fleeing from China in August, 1913, when it became clear that the "second revolution" was a failure. Having previously suffered so many reverses, he was by no means overcome by that of 1913. In Japan he proceeded to a reorganization and revivification of the Kuomingtang. From that country he sent to China numerous agents to work in the provinces against Yuan, and encourage those of his followers who had remained to continue undaunted in their plans for reform and revolt.

According to Dr. Paul Reinsch, American minister in Peking at this period, the Japanese minister warned Yuan on the occasion of his presentation of the twenty-one demands that there were in Japan Chinese revolutionists "who have very close relation with many Japanese outside of the Government, and have means and influence." Mr. Hioki remarked that it might not be "possible for the Japanese government to restrain such people from stirring up trouble in China unless the Chinese government shall give some positive proof of friendship," and that the Japanese people believed that "the president is strongly anti-Japanese." Apparently he did not say, in so many words, that the Japanese had never forgotten, or forgiven, the work of Yuan in Korea, during the last two decades of the nineteenth century (1884-94), in opposition to the Japanese and their policies in that country. So astute a ruler as Yuan might be trusted to be aware of this.

One of those whom the dictator feared, but hoped to retain as a follower, was Tsao Ao, a brilliant young follower of Liang Ch'i-ch'ao, who had received his military education in Japan. On the outbreak of the revolution of 1911, Tsao had held high office in Yunnan province, which quickly rebelled, and he had encouraged Li Yuan-hung in his revolt against the Manchus. He had shortly afterward become the military governor of Yunnan. In the revolt of 1913 he had taken no part, but Yuan feared him, and, in accordance with his policy of keeping in the capital all who might be dangerous, he had brought him to Peking early in 1914. Here Tsao had been given high office but no real power. Although not a follower of Sun Yat-sen, he was opposed to Yuan's monarchy scheme.

Early in December, 1915, Tsao Ao succeeded in effecting his escape from Peking; he fled to Japan, and thence to Yunnan. Here, toward the end of the month, he rose in opposition to Yuan. This outbreak was immediately followed by rebellions in other provinces such as Kweichow and Kwangsi. In a race with the troops of Yuan for control of Szechwan, and to aid General Feng Kuo-chang who was straddling the fence at Nanking, Tsao weakened his health and not long after died—not, however, without the satisfaction of having led a revolt which was to end in the failure of Yuan's monarchy scheme and the candidate's own death.

Popular opinion was almost solidly against Yuan, showing how little real had been the "elections" of a few months before. The dictator found he could not trust his own general, Feng Kuo-Chang, at Nanking. He was warned by Japan that he must not proceed with the monarchy, and he undoubtedly knew that Japanese officers were aiding his enemies in the south. Accordingly, he first postponed the enthronement and then, in

March, 1916, definitely abandoned his plans. Hoping to save his face and his position as president, even though he might no longer be dictator, he announced by edict:

. . . . Through misunderstandings the present trouble has arisen. My sincerity has not been sufficient to move the heart of the people, and my misunderstanding has not been able to read the signs of the times. It is the lack of virtue on my part, and, therefore, I have no right to blame others. . . . . All preparations for the restoration of the monarchy are stopped. Thus I hope that, by imitating the repentence and remorse of the ancients, the love and grace of Heaven will be received. We will cleanse our hearts and thoughts so that trouble will be averted and the people will obtain peace and tranquillity.

Opposition to Yuan did not lessen with the abandonment of the monarchy scheme. By mid-April Yunnan, Kweichow, Kwangsi, Kwangtung, and Chekiang had announced their independence. In the following month Szechwan followed suit. Demands were reiterated that Yuan should resign office. This he refused to do, although he proceeded to a reorganization of a responsible cabinet under Tuan Ch'i-jui, one of his military followers who had refused to support the monarchy scheme and fled from Peking. Yuan retained only military control. Early in May the opponents of Yuan—Sun and Huang Hsing had ere this returned from Japan—chose Vice-President Li Yuan-hung as president of the southern provinces which had declared independence of Yuan's government. The dilemma was ended by the death of the would-be emperor on June 6, and the fourth phase in China's revolution came to an end.

The first attempts at fundamental change in 1898; the later attempts of the Manchus to bring in a constitutional monarchy; the October, 1911, revolution and the temporary rise to power of Sun; and, finally, the dic-

tatorship of Yuan Shih-kai have now been traced. The
significance of Yuan's rule depends a great deal upon the
point of view of the interpreter. By many, his failure to
consummate his plans for the monarchy has been
mourned; by others, of course, he is looked upon as
nothing more than a traitor of reckless personal ambi-
tion. It would appear that no decision on this matter is
possible since the basis for such does not exist. By this is
meant that no decision can be made without knowing
what the course of Yuan's rule would have been had be
succeeded. Had he been able to go on for a period of
years, bring peace and gradually modernize the country
under many of the old forms, which the people understood, it would appear that that would have been best.
There is, however, no proof that if Yuan had been successful in instituting the monarchy he would have modernized the country; on the contrary, the bribery, assassination, and treachery which characterized his rule
might serve to indicate that his dynasty, had his family
succeeded him on the throne, would have been only a
repetition of that of the Manchus. In this case the revolution would merely have been stopped for a time to
break out more violently than before at a later period.
One thing stands out clearly from this strong man's rule,
and that is that the idea of the monarchy was greatly
weakened. The failure of as powerful an individual as
Yuan to restore the throne made it unlikely that any
other could succeed. Thus, one more step toward the
modernization of the country was taken under, and
despite, autocratic rule.

CHAPTER IV

THE WAR LORDS, 1916–28

THE death of Yuan, taken in conjunction with the conditions which prevailed in China in 1916, let loose forces which have controlled the country in large part to the present day. The dictator's disloyalty to his oath of office as president of the republic; his attempt to make himself emperor; the wasting of public funds, raised at home and abroad; the growth of the powers and numbers of provincial military governors, known as *tuchuns*, *tupans*, *tutuhs*, and *tulis*, and their satellites; the determination of Dr. Sun Yat-sen, and his Kuomingtang followers, to rule as much of China as possible, and to set up a real republic and establish new social institutions—all united to render confusion worse confounded. Mention has been made of the determination of Yuan to substitute his own military supporters for those of the 1911 revolution in the provincial governorships, and of the part this played in bringing about the "second revolution" in the summer of 1913. A number of these military followers of Yuan were the products of the Paoting Military Academy, a training school for officers which he had established at Paoting-fu, in Chihli province, in connection with his army reforms toward the close of the nineteenth century.

The *impasse* between the north and south at which the country had arrived at the time of Yuan's death was

solved by the succession to the presidency of Li Yuan-
hung, the leader at Wuchang in the October revolution
of 1911, who had been elected vice-president at the time
of Yuan's election as president in 1913. President Li
had been chosen to head the government set up by
Yuan's opponents on the collapse of the monarchy
scheme. He was a believer in a constitutional republic
and willingly gave another chance to the parliamentarians to apply their theories. Early in August, 1916,
they were reconvened in Peking and, shortly afterward,
a cabinet was formed under the leadership of Yuan's
premier, General Tuan Ch'i-jui. Shortly afterward Parliament elected as vice-president General Feng Kuo-
chang, who had held the balance of power during the
rebellion of 1915 against Yuan. The country now
entered upon a remarkably complicated interplay of
personalities and politics. There was the long-standing
question of the relation of Peking to the provinces, that
is, of provincial autonomy versus a centralized government; there was the question of north versus south,
which had been so clearly manifested during the régime
of Yuan; there was also the interrelation of President Li,
Premier Tuan, and Parliament.

The new president and his premier differed almost as
radically as had Yuan and the southerners. Li had no
desire for autocracy or military dictatorship; he was a
constitutionalist and believed in consultation with Parliament. Tuan, on the contrary, was distinctly a militarist; backed by men of the Peiyang military party, he
considered that he, and not the president, should be the
source of power and influence, and he had little use for
the parliamentarians. Tuan was concurrently minister

of war. The occasion of the main dispute between President Li and Premier Tuan was the breaking of diplomatic relations with Germany on March 14, 1917, and the declaration of war upon that country which followed five months later.

Toward the end of April (1917) Premier Tuan assembled in Peking a conference of military governors or *tuchuns*. This was done largely to force Parliament to declare war on Germany, which Tuan was convinced would be for the best all around, and which would strengthen his own position. While the *tuchuns* were in Peking a mob threatened Parliament; and it shortly developed that this mob had been composed of Tuan's soldiers. Whereupon Tuan's colleagues resigned, and Parliament declared that it would take no action with reference to war as long as Tuan remained premier.

In the meantime, Parliament had been working on a constitution—work which, it will be remembered, had been interfered with by the late President Yuan. This document outlined the powers of a strong Parliament, a moderately strong president, and a weak premier and cabinet. The premier's convention of *tuchuns* expressed itself as "greatly shocked" at such a document, and declared that Parliament ought to be dismissed unless changes were made at once. The *tuchuns* left Peking on May 21; two days later President Li, refusing to dismiss Parliament, dismissed his premier instead. Tuan's *tuchuns* of the Peiyang military party now came to his aid, and announced that the provinces under their control, namely, Fengtien, Chihli, Shantung, Hupeh, Anhwei, Chekiang, and Fukien, were independent of the parliamentary government of Li in Peking.

Without military power of his own to offset that of Tuan and his supporters, Li called upon that loyal old reactionary, Chang Hsun, who had been forced out of Nanking in December, 1911, to come north to mediate and save the country. Chang Hsun was located in northern Kiangsu province where he had twenty thousand troops who still treasured their queues as symbols of loyalty to the empire. It quickly became evident that there were drawbacks to support from Chang Hsun; the latter at once demanded the dismissal of Parliament, for which he had little more use than Tuan and the Peiyang militarists. Having no recourse but to comply, President Li dismissed Parliament by edict on June 12 (1917). The parliamentarians fled southward to Shanghai and Canton.

On June 15 Chang Hsun reached Peking, contemporaneously with the arrival of the 1898 reformer, Kang Yu-wei. Chang Hsun now decided to save the country by restoring to the throne the twelve-year-old Manchu emperor, who still maintained his shadowy court in the northern part of the Forbidden City. This dramatic event occurred at four o'clock on the morning of July 1. The restoration was for less than two weeks. From his refuge in the Japanese legation President Li refused a dukedom and, likewise, declined to resign the presidency. Premier Tuan and his supporters were again horribly shocked, especially at Chang Hsun's proposed division of the spoils, and set to work to undo Chang Hsun's work as king-maker. Vice-President General Feng Kuo-chang declared he had no connection with the movement, and all but three of the provinces declared in favor of the maintenance of the republic.

On July 12 fifty thousand republican troops attacked the capital. Chang Hsun fled to the Dutch legation— Kang Yu-wei having a few days earlier taken refuge in that of the United States. The boy-emperor retired again to the purple twilight of the Forbidden City, and Premier Tuan returned from Tientsin. President Li declined to continue in office and was followed on August 1 by Vice-President Feng Kuo-chang as acting president for the remainder of Yuan Shih-kai's five-year term. This would expire in October, 1918.

Feng Kuo-chang and Tuan Ch'i-jui belonged to rival cliques of the Peiyang (or northern) military party which had dominated Parliament in the later part of Li Yuan-hung's régime. Feng headed the Chihli faction, while Tuan controlled the Anhui clique. The Kuomintang was, of course, opposed to both groups. Feng and Tuan got along with each other no more smoothly than had Li Yuan-hung and Tuan. Tuan was determined that Feng Kuo-chang should not be elected substantive president on the expiration of the term of office which he was filling out. Accordingly, he convened in Peking a packed Parliament, known as the "*tuchuns*' parliament." This body, in October, 1918, elected to the presidency Hsu Shih-chang, a foster-brother of Yuan Shih-kai, who had served the latter during his presidency. Hsu was an elegant mandarin of the old school who had been the last imperial viceroy of Manchuria. He was elderly and of no great force of character.

During the administration of Hsu Shih-chang, which lasted until June 2, 1922, there were three outstanding cliques in the north. These were the Anfu Club (*An* for "Anhui" and *Fu* for "Fukien"; also *An* for "peace" and

Fu for "joy"), headed by Premier Tuan; the Fengtien clique, headed by Chang Tso-lin; and the Chihli clique, controlled by Tsao Kun, the *tuchun* of Chihli—whose headquarters were at Paoting-fu, southwest of the capital—and his leading general Wu Pei-fu. To maintain, and expand, his influence Tuan relied upon extensive and numerous loans from Japan which were offered in exchange for the strengthening of Japan's grip on China's natural resources. The bartering of these aroused the most bitter resentment and criticism on the part of the Chinese intelligentsia, especially the students. The latter were aroused to intense indignation by the success of the Japanese representatives at the Peace Congress in Paris and the provisions incorporated in the Versailles Treaty. They organized into student unions and became the outstanding critics of the Anfu group. So powerful did they become—backed as they were by prominent merchants and bankers—that, during the summer of 1919, they were able to force the resignation of three Anfu officials who were accused of being especially Japanophile and who fled to Japan for refuge.

In the following summer, 1920, the Fengtien and the Chihli factions united to overthrow the Anfu group. Only a few engagements were necessary to effect the rout of the Anfu followers of Tuan. Many of them took refuge in the Japanese legation, while Tuan himself retired from the cares of office to private life and the study of Buddhism. The lead in the fighting, and the chief burden of generalship, was assumed by General Wu Pei-fu, Tsao Kun's subordinate, but the division of the spoils was between Tsao Kun and Chang Tso-lin, Wu Pei-fu being largely ignored. As a result there was no love lost between Wu and Chang, and the seeds of another war were sown.

For almost two years, from the summer of 1920 to the spring of 1922, Peking was controlled by a Chihli-Fengtien government in which Chang Tso-lin, the war lord of Manchuria, held the greater share of the power. This he wielded in his own interests rather than those of his country. By the end of April, 1922, Chang decided to crush Wu Pei-fu of the Chihli clique before the latter should grow too powerful. His decision was dilatory as events quickly demonstrated. At first successful, Chang was soon forced to retreat to the Great Wall where it comes down to the sea at Shan-hai-kwan.

To his aid Wu called Feng Yu-hsiang from Shensi. The star of the latter had first shone clearly in the Anfu-expulsion war of two years before. At the time the war began in 1922 between Wu and Chang, Feng was in Shensi province, of which he was at the time acting military governor. His troops were by all odds the best trained and disciplined in China. By forced marches Feng went to the aid of Wu, sending half his army directly to participate in the struggle against Chang Tso-lin while the other half guarded Wu's communication with the Wuhan area whence came Wu's supplies.

Chang's expulsion from China proper, in the spring of 1922, left Wu Pei-fu real master of North China. In an attempt to gain the favor of Wu, the defenseless and powerless President Hsu proceeded to deprive Chang Tso-lin of his offices. Chang immediately declared himself independent of Peking, which in reality, like the other war lords of this period, he had long been. For President Hsu and his corrupt and effete government

Wu Pei-fu felt only contempt which he did not bother to conceal. Appreciating the hopelessness of his position, the president resigned office early in June (1922) and retired to Tientsin—like Tuan Ch'i-jui—to pursue studies in Buddhism.

Li Yuan-hung had for almost five years been living in Tientsin, which proved itself a veritable haven for retired, resigned, and ousted officials. He was now persuaded, apparently much against his will and better judgment, to resume the burdens of the presidency in Peking. He seized the opportunity to make clear his condemnation of the war lords and their doings in recent years. Wu Pei-fu hoped that the restoration of Li Yuan-hung might bring unity to the country by winning the support of the southern provinces. Parliament, which Li had been forced to dissolve at the orders of Chang Hsun in 1917, was now reconvened on August 1, 1922.

Meanwhile, the war lord Tsao Kun, of Chihli, Wu Pei-fu's superior in rank, was harboring not very well-concealed ambitions to occupy the presidential chair in Peking which his friend Yuan Shih-kai had first held. Tsao Kun had aided Yuan Shih-kai in the drilling of modern troops before the fall of the Manchus and had supported him against the southerners. In 1917 he had worked with Tuan Ch'i-jui to prevent the successful carrying-out of Chang Hsun's plans for the restoration of Manchu rule. Now he felt that as senior militarist in the north he should be elected president of China. Two things were necessary: to expand the power of the Chihli militarists, and to gain the support of the parliamentarians who enjoyed the constitutional right of electing the president. The military successes of Wu

Pei-fu had accomplished the first while bribery on a magnificent scale accomplished the second. It was necessary, of course, to get rid of President Li. This was accomplished by Tsao's supporters bringing about strained relations between the president and Generals Wu Pei-fu and Feng Yu-hsiang. The troops of the latter, and the Peking police, were permitted to stage a demonstration as a result of which President Li fled from Peking to Tientsin on June 13, 1923—one year and two days after his resumption of office.

Tsao's followers assumed control of the capital until the necessary completion of the bribery of Parliament could be accomplished. Parliament during its second attempt at rule had been no more successful than it had been before its dismissal by Yuan Shih-kai. If anything could serve as a justification for Yuan's dismissal of that august body in 1913–14, it would be the disgraceful actions of this group of men during President Li's second term of office. Factional strife prevented anything being done; there were scenes of wild disorder; finally, its members sold their votes to Tsao Kun in an election on October 5. It was generally believed that Tsao Kun spent fifteen millions of dollars (silver) in bringing about his accession to office which he assumed on October 10, 1923. On the same date the new "president" promulgated another "permanent" constitution.

The expulsion of Chang Tso-lin from China proper in 1922 did not end the quarrel between him and Wu Pei-fu, but international problems, including the danger for a time, in the spring of 1923, of foreign intervention, prevented a renewal of the war. By the summer of 1924, however, Wu and Chang were ready to renew their struggle. Chang was master of all the revenues in Manchuria, with the exception of the customs, and he had added several thousand White Russians to his force. Wu Pei-fu, leaving politics mainly to his patron, Tsao Kun, had concentrated on a campaign of unification of the country by force, and was at this time overlord, in a military sense, of most of China proper, except Chekiang and the three southernmost provinces—Kwangtung, Kwangsi, and Yunnan.

The conflict between Wu and Chang, the super-*tuchuns*, was opened in the last week of August, 1924, with a war between the *tuchuns* of Kiangsu and Chekiang for possession of Shanghai which, with its arsenal and its illicit opium revenues, was a supremely desirable prize. The *tuchun* of Kiangsu, Ch'i Hsieh-yuan, was an ally of Wu Pei-fu; the ruler of Chekiang, Lu Yung-hsiang, was allied with Chang Tso-lin. In declaring war upon Peking, Chang Tso-lin denounced the "wicked régime" of President Tsao Kun and Wu Pei-fu, and referred to them as the "people's traitors." The Peking coterie retorted that Chang Tso-lin was a "disturber of the peace whom the government is obliged to suppress by force."

The seeds of disloyalty so generously sown by Yuan Shih-kai had sprung up a hundred fold, and a fine crop of treachery was harvested in the two war areas of 1924. The *tuchun* of Chekiang was overcome by the insubordination and treachery of his own underlings and was forced to flee to Japan, whence he went northward to join his ally, Chang Tso-lin, in Manchuria. In the north Chang was threatening Peking overland by way of Jehol and Shanhaikwan. By treachery, according to general report, Fengtien troops broke through one of the gates in the Great Wall twenty miles west of Shanhai-kwan early in October. To stem Chang Tso-lin's Feng-tien invaders at Jehol, Wu Pei-fu dispatched, on September 23, Feng Yu-hsiang, whom he had earlier attempted in vain to send to the aid of the *tuchun* of Kiangsu in the southern area of warfare. There had been doubts for some time of the loyalty of Feng to his overlord, Wu. Before his departure for Jehol the so-called "Christian general" had intimated to his friends his dislike of the task set for him, and he had declined medical supplies for his army, stating that they were unnecessary.

On the morning of October 23 (1924) Peking received a shock such as it had not experienced since the coup d'état of Chang Hsun in the summer of 1917. General Feng Yu-hsiang had suddenly brought back his army from Jehol, covering one hundred miles in thirty-six hours. Seizing Peking, he declared himself in favor of peace. He charged the president, Tsao Kun, with bribery and proceeded to imprison him in his palace; he ordered the arrest of the parliamentarians who had lent themselves to Tsao's nefarious schemes by accepting bribes. The foreign minister, Mr. Wellington Koo, fled from the capital, disguised, it was reported, in women's clothes.

On learning of Feng's treachery, Wu, with a small contingent of picked troops, hastened back to Tientsin, expecting reinforcements from the south. He quickly learned that his communications were to be cut by the Shantung and Shansi *tuchuns* and that no help could reach him from Central China. Chang Tso-lin's forces, breaking through the Great Wall, cut Wu's communications with his forces in and near Shanhaikwan. With a reward for his capture dead or alive, Wu did not flee to a treaty port or to Japan, as most republican officials and revolutionists have done in adversity. With a few thousand soldiers he took refuge on his own ships and sailed to the Yangtze, proceeding thence to Nanking and later to Hankow, and Loyang in Honan, his old headquarters.

On October 23 the organization of two national armies under Feng Yu-hsiang as inspector-general was announced. These were known henceforth as the Kuominchun, the National People's army. On the next day mandates were issued ordering that fighting should cease and dismissing Wu Pei-fu from his office of commander-in-chief of the "expeditionary force for the suppression of the rebels." On October 31 a mandate announced the appointment of a new cabinet. On November 2 President Tsao Kun announced his resignation from the office which had cost him so much and brought him such humiliation. This resignation signalized the fall of the Chihli clique, but it did not result in Tsao's being allowed his freedom. He remained a prisoner in Peking until April, 1926.

The executive functions were now performed for three weeks by a so-called "governing cabinet," which signalized its tenure of power by bringing to an end the court of the boy-emperor, Hsüan Tung. Since 1912, except for the few days' restoration in 1917, the imperial Manchu household and its immediate followers had maintained themselves in the northern section of the Forbidden City in accordance with the abdication agreement of that year. On November 5, 1924, officers and soldiers of the national army appeared at the imperial palace, demanding that the Emperor should resign his title. On the same day he was requested to agree to a revised favorable-treatment agreement before three o'clock in the afternoon. This he refused to do, and withdrew to the home of his father, Prince Ch'un. He escaped thence a few weeks later to the Japanese legation, and from there fled for refuge in Tientsin. The treatment accorded to "Mr. Henry Pu-Yi," as the former emperor was now called, made a far from favorable impression in and outside the capital. The British, Japanese, and Dutch ministers called at the Foreign Office for assurances of the safety of the young man.

Three reasons have been generally assigned for Feng's coup against the imperial household: first, the danger of another attempt at restoration—perhaps by Chang Tso-lin—as long as the one-time ruler remained immured in the Forbidden City; second, a bid for support from the soviets, and from the party of Dr. Sun Yat-sen, the Kuomingtang; third, the need for funds to be realized from curios in the imperial palaces. The expulsion of the Emperor was a shock to both Chinese and foreigners generally. It was one more break with the past, the final repudiation, apparently, of an ideal of government held in China for some three thousand years and another blindly taken step into an unknown future.

Having overturned Wu Pei-fu and evicted the Manchu emperor, Feng Yu-hsiang journeyed to Tientsin to confer with Chang Tso-lin and the old Anfu leader, Tuan Ch'i-jui. Since his overthrow in 1920 the latter had resided in Tientsin. An agreement had been

made between him and Chang Tso-lin that in case
Chang should be victorious, Tuan would aid in a political reconstruction. After a five-day conference of the
three leaders Feng Yu-hsiang, Tuan Ch'i-jui, and Chang
Tso-lin, Marshal Tuan agreed to go to Peking as provisional chief executive. At last Tuan had the position
of head of the state which, to all appearances, he had
coveted since the first administration of President Li
Yuan-hung in 1916. Tuan assumed office on November
24 (1924). His provisional cabinet contained Anfuites
for the most part, not a portfolio being assigned to the
friends of Feng Yu-hsiang.

Although Feng had not been notably successful in
the Tientsin conference, he was, nevertheless, far from
being a spent force. On the establishment of Tuan's government Feng "resigned" his military commands and
retired for a period to the hills a few miles from Peking,
announcing his determination to travel and study
abroad. In reality he still controlled his armies—and his
armies controlled Peking. This was shown by the precipitate flight of Marshal Chang Tso-lin from Peking in
the early hours of December 2, but a little more than a
week after the establishment of Tuan's government.

Not to be outdone in the matter of ostentatious self-
effacement, Marshal Chang now followed Feng's precedent and "resigned" his titles. Chief Executive Tuan
naturally declined to accept the resignation of two such
distinguished leaders as those who formed the horns of
his governmental dilemma. His government abolished
the old titles of Feng and Chang and gave them new ones.
Instead of *tuchuns* they now became *tupans*, but the
rose under another name was as fragrant as before. Feng

was now frontier defense commissioner for the north-west; Chang, frontier defense commissioner for the northeast. Feng withdrew to Kalgan, northwest of Peking, from whence he could dominate the capital; Chang continued to rule Manchuria which he had held since 1911.

Feng and Chang were the rulers of buffer states which were intimately connected with international politics, especially those of soviet Russia and Japan. As early as February, 1925, a preliminary agreement was entered into between Feng Yu-hsiang and Russian agents; three months later a definite agreement was negotiated by which arms and ammunition were transported from Siberia across Mongolia, by way of Urga, to Kalgan. By the spring of 1925 preparations for war were being made by Feng and Chang. Chang moved his armies southward and himself proceeded to Tientsin.

Following the war of 1924, between the military governors of Kiangsu and Chekiang, another war lord had risen above the horizon in East-Central China. This was Sun Ch'uan-fang, an ally of Wu Pei-fu's ally, Tuchun Ch'i of Kiangsu. General Sun Ch'uan-fang was in Fukien province, to the south of Chekiang. He was expected to come to the aid of Tuchun Ch'i but he waited instead, and, when the opportunity presented itself, he pushed northward to seize Chekiang for himself. After the breaking of Wu Pei-fu in the war of the autumn of 1924, Chang Tso-lin's Fengtien forces pressed southward and controlled the railway line from Tientsin to Shanghai. By the autumn of 1925, a year later, Feng Yu-hsiang and Sun Ch'uan-fang had made an alliance against Chang Tso-lin. Between October 17 and No-

vember 16 (1925) Sun Ch'uan-fang pushed northward
with his armies and drove Chang Tso-lin's Fengtien
troops from Kiangsu and Anhui provinces into Shantung. Feng hoped that in an attempt to hold his position in the rich areas of East-Central China, from Tientsin to Shanghai, Chang would advance south of Tientsin
giving Feng a chance to dash eastward to that city and
cut Chang Tso-lin's communications with Manchuria,
the base of power and supplies. Instead of moving south
to fall into Feng's and Sun's trap, Chang moved his
main forces in two lines toward Tientsin and toward
Jehol, thereby causing Feng to withdraw from Peking,
and to agree at Tientsin to a truce.

Treachery, which has so noticeably characterized the
military struggles of the republican era in China, was
again evidenced by the publication, on November 27
(1925), of a joint declaration of war upon Chang Tso-
lin by Feng Yu-hsiang and Kuo Sung-ling. The latter
was a trusted general of Chang's, in command of the
latter's choicest troops. The struggle which followed
was one in which Russia and Japan were vitally concerned. Since Chang could not have maintained his
tenure in Manchuria without Japanese backing, his
overturn in Manchuria would have meant the weakening of Japan's position therein. The growth of Russian
influence in Manchuria through Feng Yu-hsiang as a
channel would have been proportionately great. The
relations between Chang Tso-lin and the Japanese had
for some months, however, been less cordial, the result
being that when Kuo Sung-ling rebelled against Chang
Tso-lin in November, Japanese sympathies were for a
time divided, and there was a period of hesitation on

their part which came near ruining Chang. During the first three weeks Kuo was successful, but at the moment when it appeared that Chang had collapsed and Mukden must fall to Kuo, the Tokyo government made known its plans to reinforce the garrisons of the South Manchuria Railway, under its control, and to maintain the neutrality of the railway zone. This made it apparent that ultimately Japan would aid Chang Tso-lin. A crushing defeat was administered to Kuo on December 23, the general and his wife being captured and executed and their bodies exhibited in Mukden on December 25.

Simultaneously with Kuo's defeat Feng's armies succeeded in expelling the Fengtien troops from Tientsin and capturing that city. But the failure of Kuo to oust Chang from Mukden, the capital of Manchuria, robbed Feng's victory of any real value and paved the way for the consummation of an alliance against Feng of Wu Pei-fu and Chang Tso-lin, the super-*tuchuns* who had warred against each other only a year earlier. Feng Yu-hsiang now found it advisable to retire for the nonce from public life. Leaving his Kuomin armies to the leadership of subordinates, he prepared to journey to Moscow. Before this, however, difficulties had arisen of a serious international nature.

In the campaign between the Kuominchun and the forces of Chang Tso-lin and Wu Pei-fu, the Kuominchun in control of the Taku forts, which guard the entrance to Tientsin from the sea, fired upon Japanese gunboats and foreign merchant vessels and prevented their freedom of navigation in and out of Tientsin. By the protocol of 1901, following the Boxer outbreak of 1900, China is required to maintain free access to Peking from the sea. Accordingly, on March 16, 1926, the min-

isters of the protocol powers presented to the Peking
Foreign Office and to the contending leaders in the civil
war an ultimatum. This demanded the cessation of, and
preparation for, hostilities in the Tientsin-Taku Bar area
and the stoppage of interference with foreign shipping.
The provisional government of Tuan Ch'i-jui was given
until noon of March 18 to reply. Twelve hours before
the expiration of the ultimatum Peking acceded to the
terms laid down and, as far as the foreign powers were
concerned, the incident was closed.

Not so, however, as concerned Peking itself. The students there were aroused by radical leaders, both
Chinese and Russian, to protest against the ultimatum
and its acceptance by the provisional government.
Some thousands of them demonstrated before the Foreign Office, demanding severance of relations with the
protocol powers. They then proceeded to the residence
of the provisional chief executive, Tuan Ch'i-jui, and
also to the ministry of the navy. The violence of their
actions caused Tuan's bodyguard to fire upon them,
killing more than thirty and wounding many more,
several of whom later succumbed.

The Kuominchun evacuated Tientsin on March 22,
1926, and retreated to Peking and Nankow. In April
they evacuated the capital, withdrawing to the northwest, where they strengthened themselves by importing
supplies from Siberia and arranging for reinforcements
from Mongolia in case of need. Marshal Feng Yu-
hsiang now journeyed to Moscow, where he was received
with honor and observed conditions under soviet rule for
several months.

The withdrawal of Feng's armies from Peking was followed by the arrival of Fengtien, Chihli, and Shantung

troops in April, 1926. Chief Executive Tuan Ch'i-jui, now very unpopular for his severe methods in quelling student riots, fell from power as he had in 1920, and again took refuge in Tientsin. President Tsao Kun was at last released and immediately resigned the presidency.

Tsao's resignation and that of Tuan Ch'i-jui left Peking to enjoy a "vacancy of power," as far as the presidential office was concerned. A Committee of Public Safety functioned for some weeks while Marshal Chang Tso-lin and Marshal Wu Pei-fu differed on the type of government which should be instituted. In order to maintain the theory of constitutional continuity, while lacking a president, the device of a regency cabinet was hit upon. Accordingly, the powers, through their legations in Peking, were happily enabled to continue the fiction of maintaining recognition of the government in Peking as the one which represented China.

On December 2 (1926) Marshal Chang Tso-lin assumed the office of commander-in-chief of the partially reorganized northern armies, now known as the Ankuochun, or "tranquillity restoration" army. A little more than six months later—in June, 1927—Marshal Chang Tso-lin formally instituted a dictatorial military government with himself as *tai-yuan-shuai*, or dictator. This government he maintained as the government of China, in the face of protests from the southerners, until June 3, 1928, when the approach of the Nationalists and their northern allies caused him to withdraw from Peking to Manchuria, where, as he entered Mukden a few days later, he was murdered by a bomb placed mysteriously in a position to wreck his train.

CHAPTER V

SUN YAT-SEN AND THE NATIONALIST MOVEMENT

HAVING traced the revolution in its military and political phases in North China from the death of Yuan Shih-kai, in 1916, to the death of Chang Tso-lin, in the summer of 1928, it now becomes necessary to survey the developments in China south of the Yangtze during approximately the same period. This area, too, suffered from wars between provinces and rival *tuchuns*, and from bandit depredations. In the north the thread of unity was the maintenance of a conservative, theoretically constitutional, government in Peking presided over by a president, with or without Parliament. In the south a liberal-revolutionary government, under the ideological, and at times actual, leadership of Sun Yat-sen and his revolutionary followers, struggled to maintain itself at Canton with the perennial hope of being able to overcome the conservative northerners and establish a progressive republican government for all China.

On the dissolution of Parliament in Peking by President Li Yuan-hung in June, 1917, its members betook themselves to Canton. Thither also went Sun Yat-sen to become generalissimo of the rebellious southern provinces, and to continue the struggle for constitutional government. The government of Sun as generalissimo lasted but a few months on account of opposition to him personally and strife among themselves of the military leaders of the southern and southwestern provinces.

In January, 1918, a directorate of seven members was established at Canton to head a southern constitutionalist government. The seven directors were Sun Yatsen, Wu Ting-fang, T'ang Shao-yi, Tsen Shun-hsuan, Lu Yung-ting, T'ang Chi-yao, and Admiral Liu Pao-yi. Of several of these mention has earlier been made. The territory over which the directorate was supposed to exercise control included the three southernmost provinces of Kwangtung, Kwangsi, and Yünnan, the two neighboring provinces of Kweichow and Szechwan, and parts of Hunan, Kiangsi, and Fukien—in a word, the greater part of China south of the Yangtze and, in the case of Szechwan, some north of that river.

Although China became a participant in the World War in 1917, she remained at war with herself: the southern government fought the northern, and various provinces and *tuchuns* carried on more or less private wars. When the time came to appoint delegates to the Peace Congress at Paris, the governments at Canton and Peking, after some hesitation, were able to agree on the personnel of the Chinese delegation. The fact that this delegation did not represent a united China greatly weakened its position. The result was bitter disappointment to the Chinese people and their friends, with consequent added impetus to revolution.

At this time were organized the student unions previously mentioned. To the student movement much of good and some of ill must be attributed during the past twelve years. Encouraged by merchants and bankers, students of all ages and both sexes staged demonstrations through a considerable part of the country. They addressed both peasants and townsmen; they translated, wrote, and scattered liberal, radical, and communistic doctrines among the people; they opened free schools for the poor; and they organized a powerful and widespread anti-Japanese boycott.

In these stirring times the position of Dr. Sun and the Kuomingtang left a great deal to be desired. In May of 1918 Sun had retired from Canton, owing to the opposition of southern militarists, especially that of Lu Yung-ting of Kwangsi. While Sun and his supporters, Wu Ting-fang and T'ang Shao-yi, retired to their residences in the foreign settlements of Shanghai, the parliamentarians were invited by T'ang Chi-yao to establish themselves in Yünnan and later in Chungking. Conditions changed so rapidly that before they arrived at either meeting place they were invited back to Canton. Attempts made in February, June, and September, 1919, to heal the breach between north and south by the conference method failed. On neither side of the Yangtze could unity be enforced.

The failures of Dr. Sun to maintain himself in the south, and his betrayals from time to time by those who professed to be his followers and members of the Kuomingtang, brought him into somewhat low repute. For the rise of the student movement he and his party were not responsible. Down to 1919 the Kuomingtang, in spite of its name, could scarcely be considered to be a national party; it was in the main a Cantonese party, or, at all events, a southern party, and was composed largely of students educated abroad.

The city of Shanghai became one of the headquarters of the student movement, and there Dr. Sun was generally to be found in the frequent intervals when he was out of office in the south. In 1919–20 the Kuomingtang and the student movement began to join forces with the result that both were strengthened and the Kuomingtang in particular took a new lease on life. The students now studied and disseminated the ideas and the writings of Dr. Sun among all classes of people.

To President Hsu Shih-chang's overtures to Dr. Sun and the southerners to aid in the unification of the country the latter turned deaf ears. They reiterated their claims to be the repositories of the only "constitutional" power in China. The fact that the terms of office of the parliamentarians had expired worried them not at all. Like an imperial German or a Japanese budget, they held over from year to year in the absence of new arrangements.

Following a split in the Canton government in April, 1920, Messrs. Sun, Wu, and T'ang again took refuge in Shanghai; they now entered into negotiations with the northern government and, for a time, it appeared possible that north and south, Peking and Canton, might be brought together by diplomacy, and a new Parliament and president elected for all China. Before this could be carried out, however, Dr. Sun's supporters in the south overthrew his enemies in the late autumn of 1920, and he returned thither from Shanghai.

The general to whom Dr. Sun owed his return to power in Canton in 1920–21 was Ch'en Ch'iung-ming. This man had assisted in the revolutions of 1911 and 1913, and had served as minister of war in 1917 in the

Canton military government. He now ousted the Kwangsi militarists from Kwangtung, making it possible for Dr. Sun to return; as a result Ch'en became civil governor of Kwangtung and at the same time commander-in-chief of the Kwangtung forces.

Despite his devotion to constitutionalism, Dr. Sun accepted in 1921 an "election" as president of the Chinese Republic by a group at Canton of the old 1913 parliamentarians. There were but 222 votes cast in the election; of these 213 were for Dr. Sun. Inasmuch, however, as a legal quorum of Parliament was 580, and three-fourths of these must have voted for the successful presidential candidate, it is clear that Sun's election was doubly lacking in validity. Nevertheless, it served an opportunistic purpose, and Dr. Sun was enabled thereby again to raise his standard and advance the claims of the Kuomingtang.

Unfortunately for the head of the new southern government, there shortly developed a break between him and General Ch'en Ch'iung-ming. The latter disapproved the election of Sun as "president," and even more thoroughly disapproved his plans for a war against the north. There were, in addition, fundamental differences in the political philosophy of the two men. Ch'en Ch'iung-ming was a strong proponent of provincial autonomy; Dr. Sun was now strongly opposed to this, and advocated a centralized government which should cure China of civil wars and protect the country from foreign aggression. In the anti-northern military move of Sun, General Ch'en failed to participate, whereupon Sun relieved him of office and persisted in his own plans. Ch'en withdrew to Waichow, east of Canton, where he prepared to overthrow Dr. Sun with the aid of Yünnanese troops in Canton.

In the north, Wu Pei-fu, after expelling Chang Tso-lin and forcing President Hsu Shih-chang to resign the presidency in June, 1922, was working to bring about a unification of the country by restoring Li Yuan-hung to the presidency and calling upon the 1913 Parliament to return to the northern capital. The provisional constitution of 1912 was to be put into force again and the *tuchuns* were to be abolished. All these were requirements for peace set forth by Dr. Sun—but the latter would have nothing to do with Wu Pei-fu and Li Yuan-hung. Ch'en Ch'iung-ming, who was probably in alliance with Wu, and was certainly in favor of his plans, was more than ever disgusted with Sun, against whom he rebelled in June, 1922. Sun was forced to take refuge upon a warship; for almost two months he carried on the struggle against General Ch'en. In the course of the war Dr. Sun's warships bombarded the city of Canton without giving opportunity to the noncombatants to withdraw. Many were killed and a considerable part of the city was destroyed. This act did not strengthen the moral reputation of the "president of the Chinese Republic" either at home or abroad. He was ultimately forced to escape to Hongkong on a British gunboat; thence he again took refuge in Shanghai. Ch'en Ch'iung-ming canceled Sun's government, and instituted an "autonomous provisional government."

Sun next set to work to try to obtain help from various foreign sources. Canada, England, Hongkong, the United States, Germany, and soviet Russia were all appealed to in one way or another. From Russia only was he able to obtain any satisfaction. Since early 1919 appeals to China and offers of assistance had been coming in from Russia from the Russians themselves and from Chinese in that country. An appeal sent to Canton, in March of 1919, praised Dr. Sun for his perseverance in marching "at the head of Chinese democracy against the northern Chinese and foreign imperialistic governments of oppression." The Peking government was described as the "puppet of foreign bankers." The disappointment of China at Versailles was followed by sweeping and flattering offers from Moscow to return to China what had been taken from her by the "former imperial Russian government." These were followed by several special missions. If not entirely deaf to Russia's appeals, both North and South China were extremely watchful of her actions.

In mid-January, 1923, Mr. Abram Adolf Joffe, head of one of the Russian missions to China, appeared in Shanghai to confer personally with Dr. Sun. After several conferences the two issued a statement in which they declared that while both agreed that "the Communistic order or even the Soviet system cannot actually be introduced into China, because there do not exist here the conditions for the successful establishment of either Communism or Sovietism," nevertheless "most cordial and friendly" relations existed between them.

In the meantime, the plans for co-operation between Wu Pei-fu and Ch'en Ch'iung-ming failing to materialize, Dr. Sun's forces were able to expel Ch'en from Canton in January, 1923, as Ch'en had expelled Sun in the preceding summer. For the fourth time Dr. Sun became the leading figure in a South China government. The effects of his friendly intercourse with M. Joffe and the soviets quickly became apparent. A tyrannical government was set up which was based on a balancing of the military forces from Yüannan, Kwangsi, and Hunan. Public property was seized, exorbitant taxation was introduced, and taxes were collected years in advance in order to pay the forces on which the government was forced to depend. Opium dens and brothels were licensed in order to aid in financial contributions. Heavy taxes on new buildings were imposed, merchants were seized for ransom, and thousands of coolies were impressed into military service.

In September, 1923, Comrade Michael Borodin arrived from Russia to act as high adviser to the Kuomingtang. From this time dated the close co-operation of the governments of Russia and Canton which lasted until the end of the year 1927. Soviet influence was augmented by the arbitrary action of the powers—Great Britain, the United States, France, Italy, Japan, and Portugal—in sending their warships and gunboats to Canton in December, consequent upon the threat of Dr. Sun to seize the customs, the surplus revenues of which, in accordance with international agreements, were being sent to the central government in Peking. This action caused Dr. Sun to state publicly: "We no longer look to the West. Our faces are turned toward Russia."

On the advice of Borodin, and with the financial aid of Russia—to the amount of three million rubles[1]—Dr. Sun established the Whampoa Military Academy, for the training of officers to lead his armies. To help in this work some thirty Russian military experts shortly ar-

[1] Louis Fischer, *The Soviets in World Affairs*, II, 640.

rived. Others appeared later for the same, or for other, technical work.

Another evidence of the influence of soviet Russia upon Dr. Sun and the Kuomingtang was the reorganization of the latter which was entered upon in 1923. The model chosen was the Communist party of Russia, the object being the tightening of the bonds of party membership and the turning of the Kuomingtang into a powerful machine controlled by a small group of leaders. Re-registration of membership was required; the result was that many of the earlier members of the party dropped out because of disapproval of the new trend, or in disgust at the growing autocracy of the leader, Dr. Sun. Many disapproved also of the *rapprochement* between the Cantonese and the Russians.

At the First Party Congress held in Canton in January, 1924, the admission into the party of Communists, who had been growing in numbers during the past five years, was permitted. The condition of their entrance into the Kuomingtang was that they should accept the principles of the latter, not that the Kuomingtang should accept their principles. This provision may be compared to the mixing of milk and red ink with the understanding that the ink shall turn white to accommodate the milk. The entrance of the Communists greatly enhanced their power, although in appearance the Kuomingtang was strengthened. From this time of reorganization dates the extraordinary revivification of the Kuomingtang which has lasted, in part at least, to the present day. From the same time begins the trouble with communism which has lasted to the present, and which bids fair to continue indefinitely. The unhappy alliance between the groups caused trouble as early as the following August—within seven months of the consummation of the union. Protests on a considerable scale broke out in Canton against the growing power of the Communists. As a result of strife within the Kuomingtang, Sun Fo, the only son of the Kuomingtang leader, and the mayor of Canton, withdrew from the south with several of his followers.

The growing power of the Communists, the fear of Russian influence, and the autocratic actions of the government of Dr. Sun created much animosity among the merchant classes in Canton. They proceeded to centralize the organization of their volunteer corps which were functioning in some one hundred and forty towns throughout the province. In the autumn of 1924 they plotted the overthrow of Sun and the bringing in again of General Ch'en Ch'iung-ming, who was waiting a chance to expel his opponents a second time. "The United Commercial Guilds of Kwangtung Province on September 24 made public a recommendation to the overseas Chinese to withdraw their financial support from Dr. Sun, denouncing him at the same time in the strongest terms. They were supported by the Committee of the Kwangtung Gentry representing 96 districts in the province, who, meeting at Fatshan late in September, repudiated the head of the Canton government and called it 'irregularly constituted, without even the support of the sentiment and good will of the local people.' Finally, the Kwangtung Provincial Assembly, on September 30, warned the League of Nations that Sun was 'a rebel disturbing local peace, and also disturbing international good will by his misrepresentations.' In all these messages, evidence of tyrannical government was adduced."[1]

Contemporaneously with the wars in East-Central and North China between Wu Pei-fu and Chang Tso-lin and their allies, Dr. Sun, by means of labor bands organized under the leadership of the left wing of the Kuomingtang, proceeded to crush the merchant volunteer organizations in mid-October, 1924, after intercepting quantities of arms which they had imported from Europe on a Norwegian ship. The destruction of a considerable part of the wealthiest section of Canton took place, accompanied by looting and great loss of life.

Following the overturn of Wu Pei-fu and the establishment of Tuan Ch'i-jui as provisional chief executive in Peking in November, 1924, Dr. Sun was invited to go north to consult with Feng Yu-hsiang, Tuan Ch'i-jui, and Chang Tso-lin on the reorganization of the government. The Kuomingtang itself disapproved the plans of the northern war lords, although the plans outlined were similar to those which Dr. Sun himself had long stood for—at least in theory.

Whether because of his own unpopularity in Canton following the suppression of the merchant volunteer organization, his failure to bring the Kuomingtang to his own way of thinking with reference to the proposed conference in the north, or for some other reason, Dr. Sun now decided to withdraw from the south to go indirectly to Peking. He went by way of Shanghai and Japan where he delayed a considerable time. On his travels northward he fulminated vigorously, often and at length, on the shortcomings of the white race and the

[1] *China Year Book* (1925), p. 850.

imperfections of Western civilization, especially the policies of the "capitalistic powers." He denounced extra-territoriality, the "unequal treaties," and the foreign concessions and settlements which had so often given him and other defeated militarists protection.

The correct attitude to be maintained by the administrators of the foreign-controlled areas in China toward Chinese military and political refugees has long been a matter of discussion. In general, the policy has been to offer hospitality to such as long as it is not clear that they are disturbers of the peace. The arrival of Dr. Sun at his home in the French concession on November 17, 1924, following the bloody suppression of the merchant volunteers, had been preceded by considerable discussion among foreigners in Shanghai as to whether he ought to be allowed to continue indefinitely to use this refuge as headquarters for revolutionary plots. This angered the southern leader and caused him to refer heatedly to his rights and those of foreigners in Shanghai. "It is to be pointed out," said he, "to those who attempt to oppose my presence here that Shanghai is China's territory, and that we, Chinese, are hosts, and foreign residents, our guests, receiving our hospitality. This being the case, I, as a citizen of China, have every right to reside in my territory, whereas foreign residents in this country, as our guests, have no authority whatever to oppose the presence in any part of China of their hosts. If, therefore, foreigners should dare to oppose or obstruct my presence in Shanghai, I, with the support of my countrymen, am determined to take some drastic steps to deal with them. Be it remembered that we, Chinese people, are not to be trifled with so long as we dwell in our own territories. Indeed, the time has come when all foreign Settlements in our country should be abrogated; should the retrocession by the Powers concerned of their Concessions in China be delayed any longer, I am afraid that some unhappy incident will happen, for every Chinese patriotic citizen has come fully to realize that China has already been infringed upon by some of the Powers long enough—so long that she can no longer tolerate such a state of affairs."[1] The fact that this was one of the last speeches to be made by Dr. Sun gave it additional significance in the years which followed.

Indicative of the same trend of thought was the speech which Dr. Sun gave ten days later in Tokyo, at the Pan-Asiatic Congress. Referring to Russia, he declared: "Russia believes in benevolence and righteousness, not in force and utilitarianism. She is an exponent of justice, and does not believe in the principle that a minority should oppress a majority. Naturally, Russia comes to link hands with the Asiatics and breaks her family ties with the West. The Europeans, fearing that the Russians may succeed in carrying out these principles, heap condemnations upon her as a rebel against the civilized world."[2] The influence of his Russian advisers was made manifest in such statements as these. It was, indeed, clear that Dr. Sun's face was now set toward Moscow. He had entered upon his last illusion; happily for him he passed away before it could be destroyed.

[1] Quoted by and from P. M. d'Elia, *North China Herald*, CLXXVII, No. 3300 (November 4, 1930), 174.

[2] Quoted by Louis Fischer, *op. cit.*, II, 632; courtesy of Messrs. Jonathan Cape & Harrison Smith (publishers), New York and London.

CHAPTER VI
THE IDEOLOGY AND PLANS OF
SUN YAT-SEN

D R. SUN reached Peking on the last day of the year 1924. Ill at the time he arrived, he died on March 12 in the capital which had so long been held by his enemies, the Manchus, and later by his own countrymen who had opposed that for which he had stood. Immediately there began a process of apotheosization, preparations for which had been undertaken during the preceding weeks.

The Kuomingtang and China as a whole were in need of a modern hero, a leader who could be translated into an ideal and who could be made the object of a unifying hero-worship in substitution for the imperial Son of Heaven sacrificed by the republicans in 1912. For this rôle Dr. Sun was eminently qualified by his years of self-sacrificing preparations for the revolution, by his having served as first provisional president of the republic, and by his writings which were to become the charter of the Nationalist movement. Many who would not follow him in life hastened to offer Dr. Sun lip-service in death, while those who had profited by his idealism in life profited even more after his death. Alive, the revolutionary leader had made mistakes; his egotism, as well as his ideas, and the methods he had voluntarily or involuntarily adopted, had brought forth many enemies both within and without the fold of the Kuomingtang. As soon, however, as the leader was dead, his faults were glossed over and forgotten, while his ideals and plans were studied and reverenced.

A document, dated March 11, 1925, the day before Dr. Sun's death, was shortly published as the will of the late Kuomingtang leader. It reads as follows:

For forty years I have devoted myself to the cause of the people's revolution with but one end in view, the elevation of China to a position of freedom and equality among the nations. My experiences during these forty years have firmly convinced me that to attain this goal we must bring about a thorough awakening of our own people and ally ourselves in a common struggle with those peoples of the world who treat us on the basis of equality.

The work of the Revolution is not yet done. Let all our comrades follow my "Plans for National Reconstruction," "Fundamentals of National Reconstruction," "Three Principles of the People," and the "Manifesto" issued by the First National Convention of our Party, and strive on earnestly for their consummation. Above all, our recent declarations in favor of the convocation of a National Convention and the abolition of the unequal treaties should be carried into effect with the least possible delay.

This is my heartfelt charge to you.

[*Signed*] SUN WEN[1]

March 11, 1925
[Written on February 20, 1925]

Doubt has been expressed as to whether the famous will of Dr. Sun was actually composed by him, whether it was drafted by Wu Tze-hui or Wang Ching-wei and merely signed by Dr. Sun, or whether the document is an out-and-out forgery. Interesting and important as this problem is from the viewpoint of historical accuracy, the origin of the will is not at present a matter of great significance. There is nothing in the document

[1] Sun Yat-sen, *San Min Chu I*, trans. Frank W. Price, p. vii. Shanghai: The Commercial Press.

which is in any way contrary to the ideas and actions of the leader, and the will constitutes a standard of faith and idealism comparable potentially to the Apostles' Creed or the Declaration of Independence.

In schools, popular gatherings, and political meetings the will is read immediately after the calling of the assembly to order and the making of three bows to the portrait of Dr. Sun. This is followed by a three-minute silence as a means of expressing reverence for the leader, and to give opportunity for self-examination and reconsecration to the cause of the revolution and the redemption of the country. The business of the meeting is then undertaken. As a means of unifying the people, and keeping ever before them the principles of Dr. Sun and the revolution, it is a most effective instrument, and has exerted enormous influence during the past six years.

The first work mentioned in the will, the "Plans for National Reconstruction," is in reality composed of three books published at intervals, namely, *Psychological Reconstruction*, *Material Reconstruction*, and *Social Reconstruction*. The third of these, *Social Reconstruction*, is mainly a work on parliamentary law worked out by Sun as a basis for the conduct of public meetings on an orderly basis. It is of no particular value, except to indicate the belief of the writer that man is a reasonable animal who can bring change in an orderly manner by rationalization and philosophy. Despite its title it does not deal with the reconstruction of society.

The ideas expressed in the other volumes on psychological and material reconstruction date back in part to the last years of the nineteenth century and the first part of the twentieth—the period of exile following Dr.

Sun's attempt to start the revolution in Canton in 1895. Some of these ideas he had preached to the students who were members of the Tung Meng Hui in Japan in 1905 and the following years; some he had ineffectually tried to apply in China following the revolution of 1911.

The *Psychological Reconstruction* appears to have been written in 1919, although the Preface thereto is dated December 30, 1918. Under the title of *Memoirs of a Chinese Revolutionary* this volume was published in English by a London firm. It was translated into English from a Russian translation from the Chinese; certain autobiographical material was added giving an account of Sun's revolutionary career from his youth to the establishment of the republic and his assumption of the provisional presidency in February, 1912.

Several of the outstanding thoughts and plans of Dr. Sun are to be found in this volume. They did not attract widespread attention until after his death, owing largely to the failure of the leader to convert his fellow-members of the Kuomingtang to his point of view, and to the fact that little attempt was made to put them into practice until after his death. Among the ideas here expressed is the psychologically revolutionary one, from the Chinese point of view, that "action is easy, and knowledge difficult."

In the Preface to the *Memoirs of a Chinese Revolutionary* are to be found Sun's explanation of the failure of the revolution after the overthrow of the Manchus and the sufferings of the people which he attributes to the wrong thought of his fellow-revolutionists. "What was that wrong mode of thought?" he asks. "It was, in their understanding, the idea that 'actions are difficult, but knowledge is easy.' This view was first expressed by Fu-Kueh, under the Emperor Wu-Ting of the Shan dynasty, two thousand years ago. Since that time it has taken root so deep in the mind of the Chinese people that now it is seemingly difficult to tear out. My whole plan for the reconstruction of China was paralysed by this saying. . . . . I discovered that the bold mind of the Chinese revolutionaries could not outstrip their courage. The whole Chinese people was in the same position. Later I devoted myself to the study of the question of 'difficulty of action and easiness of knowledge.' I studied this question for several years, and finally came to the conviction that the old tradition was false: the exact opposite is the case. I was happy because I had understood the cause of China's stagnation. It is due to the fact that the Chinese are ignorant of many things, and not at all because they cannot act.

"The fact that, even though they have knowledge, they do not act, is due to their misconception that knowledge is easy but action difficult. Imagine that we can prove the opposite, and force the Chinese to act fearlessly. Without doubt the affairs of China will move forward considerably. The theory of Fu-Kueh is my enemy, a thousand times more powerful than the authority of the Manchu dynasty. The power of the Manchus could achieve only the killing of our bodies, but it could not deprive us of our will. The might of the theory of Fu-Kueh not only destroyed the iron will of my comrades, but deceived the millions of the Chinese people."[1] Sun's opposition to the old way of thinking of

[1] Pp. 7–9. Quoted by courtesy of Messrs. Hutchinson & Co. (publishers), Ltd.

the Chinese people based on Fu-Kueh's thought is the reason for his calling this part of his "Plans for National Reconstruction," *Psychological Reconstruction*.

The widely discussed three phases through which the Nationalist revolution must pass are discussed in the fourth chapter of the *Memoirs of a Chinese Revolutionary* entitled "Problems of the Revolutionary Reorganisation of China." So also is the outline of the five-power constitution which is at present being worked out by the Nanking national government. Says the revolutionist-philosopher: "I distinguish three phases of development of the revolution: the first, military government; the second, preparatory; the third, constitutional reconstruction.

"The first phase covers the period of destruction. In this period it is proposed to introduce martial law. The revolutionary troops must finally destroy the autocracy of the Tai-Tsing dynasty, drive out the corrupt bureaucracy, root out evil practices, get rid of unjust slavery, wipe out the poison of opium, eradicate the superstition of magic and fortune-telling, and abolish likin (internal customs duties).

"In the second phase, that of preparation, the task will be to establish local self-government and facilitate the consolidation of the power of the people, making the county the unit of local self-government, subdivided into villages and rural districts. Every county, after the enemy has been cleared from its territory and military operations have ceased, will have to publish a provisional constitution to determine the rights and duties of citizens, as well as the rights of the revolutionary government. Three years later the citizens will elect their county authority. . . . . If, after the lapse of six years, peace has been established throughout the country, all the self-governing counties will have to elect one deputy each to constitute a great National Assembly. The task of this Assembly will be to establish five Chambers, in the spirit of the 'Constitution of Five Forms,' to organize the work of government: the first administrative, the second legislative, the third judicial, the fourth examinatory, the fifth for control and inspection.

"After the adoption of the Constitution, the citizens in the counties will elect by ballot a President to organise the Administrative Chamber, and will also elect deputies to constitute the Legislative Chamber: the other three Chambers will be appointed by the President, with the agreement of the Legislative Chamber. All the Chambers are responsible not to the President but to the National Assembly. . . . . After the confirmation of the Constitution, the election of the President, and the election of the Chambers, the revolutionary government shall hand over power to the President, and the preparatory phase may be considered at an end from this moment.

"The third phase is the period of the completion of the Revolution. In this period it is proposed to achieve constitutional government. In this period the self-governing counties must begin to exercise their direct civic rights: the citizens enjoy adult suffrage in the management of their county, the right of deciding political questions, and also the right of dismissing Government officials. This is the Constitutional phase, i.e., the period in which revolutionary reconstruction is completed.

This in general outline is the scheme of revolutionary tactics which I recommend."[1]

In the preparation of his plans for *Material Reconstruction* Dr. Sun set to work immediately after the Armistice of the World War in 1918, although, as earlier stated, the material contained therein was the result of years of preparation. It was written in the English language and published in New York under the title of *The International Development of China*. The Preface is dated at Canton, April 25, 1921. A Chinese edition appeared in October of the same year. This volume outlined a system of communications vast in scope. As the writer himself remarked in his Preface: "Each part of the different programs in this International Scheme is but a rough sketch or a general policy produced from a layman's thought with very limited materials at his disposal. So alterations and changes will have to be made after scientific investigation and detailed survey."[2] However impractical in details some of the plans here set forth may be, in general they, or their substitutes, are bound to be carried out in time; it will, however, take many years to apply them as a whole.

The second of the writings mentioned in Dr. Sun's will was *The Fundamentals of National Reconstruction*, and the third was the *Three Principles of the People* or *San Min Chu I*. The former bears the date of April 12, 1924, and constitutes a summarization of and supplement to the second of the three principles, namely,

[1] *Ibid.*, pp. 120–23.

[2] Sun Yat-sen, *The International Development of China*, p. xii; courtesy of G. P. Putnam's Sons (publishers), New York and London.

democracy. The three principles outlined by Dr. Sun
are those of the people's nationalism, the people's
sovereignty or democracy, and the people's livelihood.
On these principles, concerning which he had been thinking for a generation, Dr. Sun lectured in Canton between
January 27 and August 24, 1924.

It is to be observed that the dates just mentioned—
the first months of 1924—fall within the early period of
Russian domination at Canton of Dr. Sun's South
China government. This is not, however, to suggest that
the lectures are in essence Russian in their origin. Quite
the opposite. In the main they embrace Dr. Sun's own
conclusions based on his studies and experience of many
years. Undeniably he was at the time of their delivery
under Russian influence, and this influence is to be found
in certain phrases used by him especially in his discussion of the first two of the three principles. It is erroneous, however, to consider the lectures, or the principles
embodied in them, as dictated by the Russian advisers.
What the Russians insisted upon was the preparation
and delivery by Dr. Sun of his plans and ideas which
might be used for propaganda purposes by the machinery
which the Russians were aiding him and his Chinese
followers to build up.

In the Preface to the *San Min Chu I*, translated by
Frank W. Price, are to be found the following statements: "It now happens that the Kuomingtang is being
reorganized and our comrades are beginning to engage
in a determined attack upon the minds of the people.
They are in great need of . . . . material for propaganda. So I have been delivering one lecture a week.
. . . . In these lectures I do not have the time for careful

preparation nor the books necessary for reference.[1] I can only mount the platform and speak extemporaneously. .... Although I am making additions and corrections before sending the book to the press, yet I realize that in clear presentation of the theme, in orderly arrangement of the discussion, and in use of supporting facts these lectures are not at all comparable to the material which I had formerly prepared. I hope that all our comrades will take the book .... and make it a perfect text for propaganda purposes."[2]

As mentioned above, the three principles of the people are the principle of the people's nationalism, the principle of the people's sovereignty (democracy), and the principle of the people's livelihood. In the mind of Dr. Sun the first issue—nationalism—included the struggle for international equality, self-determination for the weaker peoples, the cultivation of the best in old China, and the supplementing of this with the best from modern culture so that progress should be constant. The second issue—sovereignty—stood for participation in the government by the people, and included a differentiation between governmental power, such as election, recall, initiative, and referendum, which should be in the hands of the people, and ruling authority, that is, the judicial, legislative, executive, civil service examination, and censorship—in other words, the five-power government—which should be in the hands of the duly elected rulers. The third principle—livelihood—aimed at economic equality of the people by the equalization of

[1] Dr. Sun's library, notes, and manuscripts had been destroyed in June, 1922, on the occasion of Ch'en Ch'iung-ming's revolt against him.

[2] *San Min Chu I*, pp. xi–xii.

landholdings and the prevention of land monopoly, the limitation of private capital, and the gradual bringing-in of state capitalism. A vague and undefined socialism, but distinctly not Marxism, which he criticized and refuted in considerable detail, was the aim of Dr. Sun in his third principle.

Two facts related to the *San Min Chu I* have not received the attention they deserve: first, that a period of more than three months elapsed between the presentation of the two series of six lectures each, on "The Principle of the People's Nationalism" and "The Principle of the People's Sovereignty," and the last four lectures on "The Principles of the People's Livelihood"; and, second, that during this period a book entitled *The Social Interpretation of History*, by an American scholar, Dr. Maurice William, of New York City, fell into Dr. Sun's hands which profoundly affected his philosophy of history and revolution as presented in his analysis of the third principle.[1]

The lectures on the first and the second principles were delivered between January 27 and April 26, 1924; those on the third principle were given between August 3 and August 24. In the first two series the ideology, as well as the criticism of the great powers, presents the viewpoint of a follower of Marx; in the third series, however, a definite change of view is indicated. Dr. Sun was too securely bound to the Russian chariot by this time, and too dependent on continued support from the

[1] Cf. *ibid.*, trans. Frank W. Price, p. 382; J. W. Jenks, *Why China Repudiated Bolshevism*, a lecture delivered at New York University on February 6, 1929; Maurice William, *Sun Yat-sen versus Communism*, a mimeographed pamphlet sent to the writer by Dr. William, containing proof of the relationship between his work and Dr. Sun's third principle.

Russian revolutionists, to break with them; this is evident by the tone of his speeches in Shanghai and Japan in the last months of 1924. Nevertheless, in point after point he cites Marx only to criticize the latter's arguments and conclusions, and to advocate in their stead the theories which he had somewhat gropingly been developing for several years and which he found carefully and precisely formulated by the American thinker in the volume mentioned. In paragraph after paragraph Dr. Sun either quoted, almost word for word, or paraphrased, the arguments which he had found in *The Social Interpretation of History*. He now repudiated in reality several of his own earlier theories, without, however, directly calling attention to the fact, and rejected Marx's materialistic conception of history, the necessity for the class struggle, and the theory of surplus values, substituting therefor the system of thought which he had recently discovered in Dr. William's work.

The third series of lectures was never completed, and Dr. Sun died shortly over six months later, surrounded mainly by those who were converts to revolutionary Russian thought and sustenance. The conflict of theory to be traced between parts of the earlier and the later writings of Dr. Sun accounts in part for the split between his adherents which followed his death. What might have happened had he completed his lectures on the principle of livelihood, and, more particularly, had he lived another decade, it is, of course, impossible to opine. It is, however, an interesting matter on which to ponder. From the viewpoint of the Russians and the significance of the spread of their communistic doctrines in China, the Kuomingtang leader died not a moment too soon; it would have been better had he passed from the scene at the end of April, 1924. There would have been fewer grounds for controversy among his followers. But it was not too late for men of decision to profit by his union with the Russians during the years 1923–24; moreover, it was possible to stress the first two of the principles at the expense of the third, which is admittedly incomplete, and continue the alliance with the soviets without whose aid there was small hope of success for the Kuomingtang revolutionists.

The last of the documents mentioned in Dr. Sun's will was the manifesto issued by the Kuomingtang First Party Congress of January, 1924.[1] This document is in three parts of which the first summarizes the history of the revolution; the second outlines the three principles of the people, and calls for their dissemination among the people; and the third outlines the domestic and foreign policy to be followed by the party. The domestic policy was to follow the ideas set forth above. The foreign policy called for the taking of all steps for making China the equal of any modern state by the abolition of all limitations upon her sovereignty such as the settlements and concessions, extraterritoriality, the navigation by foreign vessels of China's coast and inland waters, and the landing and retention of foreign troops on Chinese soil. It remains to consider the development which followed the death of the leader and the rise to power of his successor, Chiang Kai-shek.

[1] Cf. *post*, chap. vii, pp. 92–93.

CHAPTER VII

THE RISE OF CHIANG KAI-SHEK AND BORODIN

DURING the period 1911–24 the Kuomingtang may be said to have been in a state of solution. The reagent which brought precipitation was soviet Russia, in the person of Comrade Michael Borodin. Without his aid, and that of his Russian colleagues, and the backing, material and ideological, of Moscow, there is little to indicate that Canton would have become anything more than it had been for many years, namely, a center of unrest and rebellious disaffection. Here for years there had been an interplay of conflicting theories and personalities which had time and again brought civil strife accompanied by plundering, burning, and the exhaustion of one of the richest areas in the country. Dr. Sun had for a generation been the leading exponent of revolutionary ideals and methods of government, but of the application of constructive measures he had shown himself all but incapable. This was owing in part to the fact that many of his closest supporters had doubted the wisdom of his plans, and had themselves been mutually jealous, suspicious, and personally ambitious. A degree of unity had been attained as long as there had been the Manchus to serve as a scapegoat for China's mistakes. When the latter were overthrown and the problems of construction were to be faced, what unity there had been had disappeared.

The middle-class characters who had been conspicuous during the revolution of 1911 had no intention of attacking an economic system with which all their interests were allied. Nor were they willing to stand aside to permit others to carry on a program of which they disapproved in essence and which they considered to be doctrinaire and impossible of accomplishment. Something of this is made clear in a letter from General Ch'en Ch'i-mei, one of the 1911 revolutionists, to Huang Shing, another of Dr. Sun's followers: "But the word that Dr. Sun inclines towards the idealistic having taken hold of our mind makes it difficult for his principles to be put into effect. Even today there are people who hold this opinion against him. But in the evidence of past events, should we attribute the great defeat of our party to the ideals of Dr. Sun, or rather to our misunderstanding of such ideals as wrong and our opposition? Because formerly we thought his ideals were wrong, and this caused our defeat, so to-day we should not lightly take his opinions as idealistic and refuse obedience, thereby giving ground for regret in the future."[1] Even more clearly was the principle stated by the leader himself at the opening of the party conference on January 20, 1924. In the course of a long address Dr. Sun observed: "Besides the two things of the reorganization of the party and the reconstruction of the country, there is another thing which we want to call your attention to. It is that the reason for the lack of solidarity in our party in former days was not because of any enemy using great power to

[1] Quoted by T. C. Woo, *The Kuomintang and the Future of the Chinese Revolution* (London, 1928), p. 34. Quoted by financial arrangement with Messrs. George Allen & Unwin, Ltd.

destroy us; it was entirely due to the fact that we destroyed ourselves; it was because the mind and discernment were too immature, often engendering senseless misunderstandings. Therefore the power of solidarity of the whole party was very much scattered, and this caused the Revolution to fail. Hereafter we must be united and of one mind. We want to offer our own wisdom and ability to the party. We are not to use our own wisdom and ability for individuals, but for the party. All of us shall be united, for party and for country, with one aim and with one step. It is only in this way that we can achieve success. . . . ."[1]

According to soviet reports, the program for the Kuomingtang adopted by the First National Congress at this time was outlined by Borodin himself.[2] As a result of a conversation with Sun in November, 1923, Borodin had obtained the promise of a promulgation of two decrees, one of which would reduce land rent by 25 per cent, and the other would organize the peasants along revolutionary lines so that they would adhere to the party and become anti-militarist and anti-imperialist. A committee consisting of Wang Ching-wei, Hu Han-min, Tai Chi-t'ao, Liao Chung-kai, and Borodin officially prepared the program. "It was based," says Fischer, "on three principles accepted by Sun Yat-sen: (1) Co-operation with Soviet Russia and the Chinese Communist Party, (2) Anti-Imperialism, and (3) A Workers' and Peasants' programme. Around this formula Borodin wrote the entire declaration. Borodin thus grafted Bolshevik determination on Chinese indifference, and the Soviet

[1] *Ibid.*, p. 39.

[2] Cf. Louis Fischer, *op. cit.*, II, 638.

civilian method on time-honoured Chinese military tendencies."[1]

Not without opposition, as earlier indicated, was the Russian domination of the Kuomingtang brought about. It was not, however, until the removal of Dr. Sun from leadership of the Kuomingtang that intra-party strife became a matter of vital concern. The death of the leader at once raised the question of succession, and gave free scope to the struggles between party factions. The unity of the party, for which Dr. Sun had pled in January, 1924, was quickly broken, owing to personal jealousies, disputes over policy, and the clever playing of one group against another by the Russian advisers while themselves enacting the rôle of mediators. Not even in the right and left wings themselves was there unanimity. At the extreme right were such men as Wang Ch'ung-hui, the country's outstanding legal authority, and C. T. Wang, a follower of Dr. Sun prior to, and during, the 1911 revolution. These men still had hopes of unifying the northern and southern elements of the country, and, for a time, co-operated with Tuan Ch'i-jui and Feng Yu-hsiang. More advanced in political principles was the Western Hills faction, so called from a conference held in the hills west of Peking in December, 1925. This group differed with the Canton groups mainly in demanding the expulsion of the Communists from the Kuomingtang and the dismissal of the Russian advisers. For daring to take such action they were bitterly denounced as mutineers; they failed to carry

[1] *Ibid.*, p. 640. Quoted by courtesy of Messrs. Jonathan Cape & Harrison Smith.

their program into effect, and were expelled from the party in the following year.

In Canton there were two aspirants for the seamed mantle of Dr. Sun, namely, Hu Han-min and T'ang Chi-yao. The former, a native of Kwangtung, had been a friend and follower of Dr. Sun since his student days in Japan in the early years of the century, and had been left in charge of affairs at Canton when Sun started northward in 1924. The latter, a native of Yünnan, was a militarist on whose Yünnanese troops Dr. Sun had depended in part during the period of his last administration in Kwangtung. In less than a week after Sun's death he assumed the title of vice-generalissimo of the Kuomingtang armies which had earlier been offered to him. This meant the military headship of the southern government, and foreshadowed a struggle with the Kwangtung troops and their leaders who resented the presence of the Yünnanese and looked upon T'ang as an ordinary *tuchun*.

Among the opponents of the Yünnan and Kwangsi militarists were the members of the Central Executive Committee of the Kuomingtang controlled by a group sometimes designated the "elder statesmen." Among these were Hu Han-min, Wang Ching-wei, and Liao Chung-kai. Wang, who had been with Dr. Sun at the last, and Liao, an American-born Chinese who was in charge of the workers' and peasants' section, were extreme radicals. Hu was not an extremist, and was opposed to the growing influence of the Russians.

Two other groups who did not see eye to eye with the temporarily powerful triumvirate were headed by Sun

Fo, the late leader's only son, and T. V. Soong, Dr. Sun's brother-in-law by his second marriage. These groups were at times referred to as the "prince" and the "uncle" factions, respectively.

Some six weeks after the death of Sun civil war again broke out in Canton. For a time the Yünnan and Kwangsi troops of T'ang Chi-yao and his adherents were successful, but in June they were driven out with great brutality and bloodshed. Strengthened by military successes, the Central Executive Committee contemporaneously expelled from the Kuomingtang all who were in sympathy with the Western Hills faction. In the meantime, on May 23, a resolution, worded by Wang Ching-wei, was passed announcing the inability of the party to join with Peking in the reorganization of the country, and calling for co-operation only with Russia. The fires of patriotism were fanned and the sympathies of the southern nationalists with communism and soviet Russia were strengthened by the Nanking Road (Shanghai) and the Shakee-Shameen (Canton) incidents of May and June (1925). In these or other brushes with foreigners a number of lives were lost on both sides; the result was the bringing-about of a state of tension in the relations of China with the great powers, and the strengthening of the influence of the extremists—Chinese and Russian —in the Kuomingtang. On the advice of the Russians mainly, British interests and nationals were concentrated upon during the next two years, although attempts to weaken the position of other foreigners were not lacking.

Early in July a Chinese soviet government was established at Canton headed by a political council and an administrative council. Overshadowing and directing this government was the Central Executive Committee of the Kuomingtang. In this reorganized Committee Messrs. Wang Ching-wei, Hu Han-min, Liao Chung-kai, and Sun Fo were for a few weeks the surface leaders. The struggle between the more moderate bourgeois and the radical Communist groups continued. Late in July several of the former, including Mr. Sun Fo, were forced to withdraw from Canton. Exerting greater influence day by day behind Wang, Hu, and Liao was Comrade Borodin. On August 20 occurred the assassination of Liao Chung-kai, minister of finance, chief of the workers' and peasants' section, and political commissar of the Whampoa Military Academy. This was interpreted by Borodin as an indication that the less radical generals such as Wei Pong-bing, who had ousted the Yünnanese, were planning to contest with the extremists the control of the party. Borodin held also that the British, who were trying to break a great strike directed against Hongkong, were implicated, as well as Hu Han-min who had long held reservations concerning the Russians, and who was ambitious to head the party which was now ruled by committees after the Russian pattern. On the plea of danger to the revolution Borodin succeeded in obtaining the appointment of a dictatorial triumvirate composed of Wang Ching-wei and Generals Chiang Kai-shek and Hsu Chung-sze. Hu Han-min was not only not appointed to membership in the supreme group but was arrested, and shortly after exiled to Moscow.

Of the three nominal rulers of Canton, Chiang Kai-shek was the least known to the public and apparently

the least significant. Hsu Chung-sze was the commander-in-chief of the Kuomingtang forces; he it was
who had defended Dr. Sun against Ch'en Ch'iung-ming
in 1923. Hsu was, of course, Chiang's military superior,
but he was suspected by the Russians; his counsels of
peace were disregarded, and he was actually powerless.
By a coup in September (1925) maneuvered by Borodin,
Chiang Kai-shek, with the aid of the Whampoa cadets
and the ten thousand Hongkong strike pickets, became
commander-in-chief of the Kuomingtang forces. Wang
Ching-wei remained in power for the nonce, but the
actual ruler was Borodin, without whose consent neither
Wang nor Chiang could act.

As has been made abundantly clear, the stars of the
Kuomingtang had long been fighting in their courses.
Not until the summer of 1925 did it become apparent
that Chiang Kai-shek's was one of the first magnitude,
and not for another two years was the fact to be made
evident. Chiang is a Chekiang man. Born in 1887 at
Fenghwa, southwest of Ningpo, he became, at the age
of nineteen, a student in the Tokyo Military College.
While there he became a follower of Dr. Sun and joined
the Tung Meng Hui which was later to evolve into the
Kuomingtang. On the outbreak of the 1911 revolution
at Wuchang he returned to China to participate in the
struggle under General Ch'en Ch'i-mei. For a time he
was one of Dr. Sun's secretaries. The failure of the
"second revolution" in 1913, and the consolidation of
Yuan Shih-kai's position, interrupted his military career,
and for a time he was in business in Shanghai. Later he
became chief-of-staff to Ch'en Ch'iung-ming. During
the struggles of Ch'en with Sun, Chiang found difficulty

in serving two masters; his earlier loyalty overcame his later and, while officially serving Ch'en, he advised Sun to attack the latter. After this Chiang again entered into discreet obscurity; then, in August, 1923, after Sun's and Joffe's *rapprochement*, he was sent by the former as confidential representative to Moscow to meet Lenin, Trotsky, and Chicherin, to study bolshevist strategy, ideology, and revolutionary technique, and to seek aid of a material nature from Moscow. Returning to China, he was appointed principal of the Russian-inspired, recently established Whampoa Academy. The protégé first of Sun Yat-sen and later of Borodin, a man of decision and iron nerve, Chiang, who was now reckoned a Communist, seized the opportunity so carefully prepared by Borodin. So successfully did the two men co-operate for the nonce that during the remaining months of the year 1925 all opposition to the Communist-Kuomingtang forces in the Kwangtung area was overcome.

Simultaneously a recrudescence of anti-Christian feeling, which had been forming during the past three years in various parts of the country, came to a head. During the next two years—and to a lesser degree and on occasion to the present day—its influence was strongly felt wherever the Nationalists intrenched themselves. To understand the basis of the anti-Christian movement numerous factors, psychological, cultural, philosophical, scientific, and personal, have to be considered. In the first place, although since the Boxer period there had been a notable recession of such feeling, and for some fifteen years Christianity and its institutions had enjoyed a very considerable degree of popularity and success from the points of view of both influence and numerical conversions, the opposition of the Confucian literati, and of the ignorant masses, to foreigners and their religion, so often manifested in the nineteenth and earlier centuries, had never entirely passed away. The assumption and demonstration that there could develop outside China ideas and institutions more efficacious than those which the Chinese had evolved were in themselves distasteful and offensive. The very presence of the missionary constituted a criticism of the native culture, and a threat to a system of life which had been in process of evolution for several thousands of years. Modern science and philosophy broke the monopoly held by the literati of the old school. In an earlier day the Christian missionary and the native convert were disliked as innovators; in a later period they are criticized not for radicalism but for conservatism. Enthusiastic, and often immature, exponents of the latest theories of the West scorn not merely Christianity but all religion, on the charge that it is a conservative and superstitious force blocking scientific and philosophical pursuit of truth.

The age-old factor of "face" is involved in the vast sums of money poured into China for the building-up of churches, hospitals, orphanages, schools, and colleges, and the direction of expenditures and management of these institutions by foreigners. The efficiency and effectiveness of these institutions as a whole in comparison with many, but by no means all, native-managed Chinese institutions is a standing criticism of the latter. The dissemination through the foreign-fostered institutions of alien ideas and religious teachings also render them suspect.

There is the unfortunate fact to be reckoned with, in addition, that the foundations of modern Christian work in the country were laid in treaties which were negotiated, directly or indirectly, in the main as a result of wars between China and the Western powers. The justice or injustice of the wars, and the wisdom, or lack of it, envisaged in the incorporation of toleration clauses for Christianity in the nineteenth-century treaties are debatable issues. That the relationship exists for good reason or bad is undeniable. This has proved an excellent weapon of attack in the hands of antireligious propagandists during the past decade.

The bolshevik ideologues, who joined forces with the southern Chinese in 1924, were not slow in availing themselves of the opportunities offered for linking up Christianity with imperialism. As long as Dr. Sun, a professed Christian, was alive little was done above the surface. Immediately after his death, however, the attack was begun in a struggle over the type of funeral which should be accorded him. His widow, herself a Christian, insisted that a religious service should be held; the result was the holding of a private Christian service before the public funeral ceremonies were carried out. With the cementing of the union of the Communist and Kuomingtang parties, and the rise of Borodin to practically dictatorial power in the autumn of 1925, the way was opened for avowed Nationalist support of an antireligious movement. As the southerners moved northward from Kwangtung toward and through the

Yangtze Valley in 1926–27, attacks upon Christian institutions and converts, with direct or indirect expulsion
of alien religious workers, took place on a grand scale.
The missionaries were dubbed "imperialists," while their
native colleagues and converts were known as the
"running dogs of the imperialists."

Although military opposition to the left clique in control of Canton had been overcome by the close of the
year 1925, the situation was full of uncertainty during
the first months of 1926. While the right wing was in
no position to overcome the left, it constituted, nevertheless, a source of danger, and no one could tell when
it might again dispute for supremacy. There was danger
to the revolution if either the communistically inspired
peasants' and laborers' unions or the militarists should
gain complete control. Not only had the members of the
Kuomingtang to fear the old-style *tuchuns;* they had
also to beware of the rising power of their own militarists. The civilian elements in the party were determined
to revert to the system of civilian control of the armies
which had prevailed in old China and which had been
broken under the republic. Between these three stools
the Kuomingtang-Communist revolution was to fall in
less than two years, carrying with it the Chinese soviet
republic of 1925–27.

The Hongkong strike was continuing during these
months, and Hongkong was suffering severely, but it
was becoming clear that Canton by itself was not a
broad enough base for a successful attack on the British
Empire of which Hongkong was but a small, if significant, part. In North-Central China, Wu Pei-fu,
against whom Dr. Sun had long thundered, was still a

power to be considered, and he was pushing southward. Moreover, his forces and territories lay between those of Feng Yu-hsiang and Canton—and, since the late autumn of 1924 at least, Feng had been toying with thoughts and agents of Moscow and Canton, and receiving aid from the former.

In addition to these general aspects of the situation there were those of a personal nature: the relations and the position of Wang Ching-wei, Chiang Kai-shek, and Borodin left something to be desired. Incidents shortly to follow showed that the two Chinese were not temperamentally fitted to play the rôles of Damon and Phintias, while the influence of Borodin was more than a little irksome to Chiang, who had no intention of serving indefinitely as a string to Borodin's bow. The degrees of Chiang's communism, patriotism, and opportunism were more than a little unclear. Quite aside from his relations with the Chinese were Borodin's connections with the soviet leaders in Moscow, who themselves were not at one. Almost from the beginning Borodin had found himself in difficulties with respect to his superiors at home. That he was the representative of a Communist-revolutionary government instead of an "imperialist" state did not prevent his finding that the aims and instructions of a government thousands of miles away from China do not always coincide with the factors with which a foreign diplomat has to deal. He was not the first to discover this, or yet the last. Trotsky and his followers wanted sovietization, and they wanted it at once. Stalin and his group were willing to make haste slowly. The third international had its own policy, which might, or might not, fit in with the foreign policy of the group in control of the Moscow government at a given moment. Borodin faced conditions which did not, he felt, warrant the immediate application of Communist theories: a nationalist, anti-imperialistic revolution was sufficient for the time being. He is reported to have remarked, "We could have seized power in Canton, but we could not have held it. We would have gone down in a sea of blood. We would have tried it if we had had a 25 per cent chance of existing for one year."[1] Events in Canton in December, 1927, demonstrated the accuracy of Borodin's diagnosis. Stalin, not Trotsky, sensed the true state of affairs in China at this time.

The influence of Russia was strengthened in January, 1926, by the convening of the Second Biennial Kuomingtang Congress at Canton. The need for effective relations with Moscow was again affirmed. Wang Ching-wei, who, a few weeks earlier, had publicly denied that he was a Communist, but had advocated the continued co-operation of Communists and Nationalists in the struggle against imperialism, was elected chairman of the Central Executive Committee. Of the thirty-six members of the new executive, however, less than one-third were sincere supporters of the Borodin régime. Wang was elected also to membership in the Political Bureau, which was composed, in addition, of Hu Han-min, now exiled to Russia; T'an P'ing-shan, a prominent Communist who had aided in the formation of the peasants' and workers' unions; T'an Yen-k'ai, a scholar-militarist who had participated in the 1911 revolution

[1] Fischer, *op. cit.*, p. 647. Quoted by permission of Messrs. Jonathan Cape & Harrison Smith (publishers), New York and London.

and later opposed Yuan Shih-kai's imperial ambitions; C. C. Wu, a son of Wu Ting-fang and who was later to become minister to Washington; Sun Fo; T. V. Soong, Mme Sun's brother who had become minister of finance on the death of Liao Chung-kai; Chu P'ei-teh, a Yünnanese follower of Dr. Sun who had retained control of his forces when the non-Cantonese forces had been expelled or butchered; and Chiang Kai-shek. It will be observed that the groups officially controlling the government were composed of men of divergent opinions.

The relations between Chiang and Borodin were now unsatisfactory. On neither the goal nor the method of attaining it could they agree, although both advocated entrance upon the northern campaign which Dr. Sun had always hoped, but never been able, to undertake. Chiang wanted to strengthen his own position, and Borodin desired a broader base for the revolution.

To line up Feng Yu-hsiang with the southerners, Borodin left Canton for the north in February (1926). Supported by C. C. Wu, T'an P'ing-shan and Chu P'ei-teh, Chiang seized the opportunity, between the fifteenth and twentieth of the following month, to carry out a coup having for its double object the breaking of the Communist grip on the party and the releasing of himself from the civilian supervision of Wang Ching-wei, the lynch-pin in the Communist-Kuomingtang soviet republic. Wang fled to Europe; a number of the Russian and Chinese radicals were arrested, several of the former being deported, and negotiations were undertaken with Hongkong looking toward the ending of the strike.

But Chiang was not yet prepared for a final break with Borodin. Gladly would he have eliminated the soviet goose, but the golden eggs were indispensable to his success. Nor were Borodin and the extreme left Kuomingtang and Communists in a position to oust Chiang and his troops with their middle-class sympathizers. Accordingly, the annulment of the marriage of convenience between the Communist party and the Kuomingtang was postponed a few months longer, and, on April 25, in order to show that he was not a right-wing reactionary, Chiang executed a second coup, this time against the right. Several of those who had advocated the stroke against the left wing now received similar treatment. Mr. C. C. Wu was forced to retire to Shanghai, while Sun Fo, to avoid a trip to Moscow, was forced to accept the relatively uninfluential post of mayor of Canton in which he was carefully supervised. The relations between Chiang and Borodin, while strained, were not broken, and Borodin continued to aid in the preparation for the northern campaign. Each hoped to derive sufficient strength from this move to expel the other.

In the meantime the breach was healed, to an uncertain extent, by the convening of the Central Executive Committee in Canton in mid-May (1926). Shortly before this Hu Han-min had returned from Moscow to Canton with Borodin, who had finished his conference with Feng in North China and returned by way of Vladivostok. The roundabout route followed by Borodin had been necessitated by the unsolicited attentions of Chang Tso-lin's agents. In Moscow, Hu had discussed Chinese affairs with the leaders of bolshevism and had obtained from them assurances that there were no objections to Communists becoming members of the Kuomingtang and supporting, temporarily, the *San Min* principles of Dr. Sun. They assumed the attitude earlier maintained by M. Joffe that China was unready for communism, and agreed to support the Nationalist revolution. Far from having been converted to communism—to the theories of which he paid a certain amount of lip-service in order to placate the radicals—Hu continued to support the aims of Dr. Sun for a Nationalist state. In spite of these maneuvers he was not able to remain long in the south. As a result of the plenary session of the Central Executive Committee, Mr. Eugene Ch'en succeeded him as acting minister of foreign affairs, and Hu withdrew to Shanghai.

Born in Trinidad, and accordingly a British subject, Mr. Ch'en had received a legal education in England and had arrived in China in 1912; two years later he renounced his British nationality. For a time he had served Yuan Shih-kai, but, after difficulties with Tuan Ch'i-jui, he had joined Dr. Sun. As a newspaper editor he had developed an anti-British attitude and demonstrated a devastating power of vituperation which preeminently fitted him for the duties which he assumed during the next sixteen months.

The chairman of the Central Executive Committee was now Mr. Chang Chin-chiang, a co-provincial of General Chiang with whom the latter had once been in business in Shanghai. The new chairman had long been a devoted friend to Dr. Sun and had given him financial assistance to the extent of his private fortune. To him was submitted, in accordance with a resolution of the Central Executive Committee, a list of Communists who had joined the Kuomingtang, but no use of this list appears ever to have been made.

CHAPTER VIII

WUHAN *vs.* NANKING

STRIFE within the party being no longer imminent, preparations were undertaken for the northern campaign. This was to be of a twofold nature—military and propagandistic, with the emphasis upon the latter. Chiang Kai-shek was officially commander-in-chief, but the plan of campaign was Russian. Some fifteen soviet military officers under the direction of General Blücher (Galens), the chief military adviser of the government, accompanied the expeditionary forces, who ultimately numbered about one hundred thousand. Of these, two corps of some twenty thousand were under Chiang. They constituted the actual Kuomingtang army which had been trained at, or by officers from, the Whampoa Military Academy. The remainder were former supporters of the *tuchuns* of the southern provinces. In each of the ten corps one or more Russians held strategic positions for military or propaganda purposes. At the head of the Political Bureau, which prepared and disseminated propaganda, was the Communist Teng Yen-ta—despite the fact that a resolution had been passed by the Central Executive Committee disqualifying Communists from the position of departmental chairman in the government. Teng had succeeded Wang Ching-wei as political supervisor of Whampoa, and had been attacked by Chiang in his coup of March 25, 1926.

Having brought Kwangtung under his control,

Chiang next gained Kwangsi. In Hunan to the north, meanwhile, General T'ang Sheng-chih had revolted against his superior, Governor Chao Heng-t'i, who was an adherent of Wu Pei-fu. By June (1926) Chiang was able to send troops to the aid of T'ang who, on July 13, took Changsha, the provincial capital. A few days earlier the main forces of the Nationalists had been officially dispatched on the northern expedition. These were preceded and accompanied by plain-clothes propagandists who preached to peasants and townsmen the principles of Dr. Sun and Lenin; scattered vast quantities of placards, pamphlets, and handbills; organized the people, willing and unwilling, into peasants' and workers' unions; and set up soviet local governments. With the official ending of the Hongkong strike on October 10 (1926), thousands of pickets were transferred to Hankow to wage economic war upon Chinese and foreign bourgeois-capitalist interests.

Part of the southern troops passed directly north through Hunan to the Yangtze; others carried the campaign into Kiangsi and Fukien, two of Sun Ch'uan-fang's five provinces. On September 6 Hanyang was treacherously surrendered to the southerners by its general, and Wu Pei-fu retreated northward. Two days later Hankow fell. Wuchang underwent a siege by Chang Fa-k'uei and his Ironsides until October 11. Heavy fighting took place in Kiangsi, but General Chiang established himself at Nanchang, the capital, early in November. Late in the month he pressed toward Hangchow, the capital of Chekiang, his native province, but not until January, 1927, did a serious invasion of this province occur. On February 18 Hang-

chow fell, and a few weeks later the collapse of Sun
Ch'uan-fang, brought about by Nationalist propaganda
and treachery in his ranks, threw the control of the rich
Shanghai area into Chiang's hands. By the end of
March the only provinces in China proper which were
definitely opposed to the Nationalists were Shantung
and Chihli, where Chang Tso-lin was still in control.

Before this, however, the inevitable break between
Chiang and Borodin, and their respective followers, had
taken place with results which were immediately disastrous to both groups. The aims and objectives of the two
leaders were diametrically opposed. Borodin planned to
base on peasant and labor unions a radical government
in Central China which should maintain close relations
with Moscow from which he was receiving direct
orders. Chiang, as he proceeded farther from Canton,
realized the need for support from the capitalist, mer-
chant-banker class whose base of power was Shanghai.
Consequent upon the Nationalist successes of the summer and autumn of 1926, an extraordinary session of
the Kuomingtang congress was convened at Canton at
Borodin's behest. At this it was decided to make Hankow the Nationalist capital, and to recall Wang Ching-
wei from his exile in Paris. Shortly afterward, Borodin
and the left-wing leaders started for Wuhan to put into
effect the resolutions of the congress. Among those constituting the nucleus of administration were Mme Sun,
Sun Fo, T. V. Soong, Teng Yen-ta, T'ang Sheng-chih,
and Eugene Ch'en. On December 11 (1926) a mass meeting, estimated by the Chinese press at three hundred
thousand, was held to welcome Borodin and his colleagues. Five hours of oratory followed during which

many antiforeign, and particularly anti-British, speeches were delivered. The following weeks were marked by anti-British and anti-Christian demonstrations on a considerable scale, including the taking over of control of the British concession at Hankow.

At his headquarters in Nanchang, the capital of Kiangsi, Chiang Kai-shek, the Nationalist generalissimo, was becoming alarmed and disgusted by the radical, communistic trend of Wuhan. On January 3, the day on which the first attack on the British concession occurred, he telegraphed a request that the Central Executive Committee of the Kuomingtang should convene in Nanchang where Chang Chin-chiang, chairman of the Central Executive Committee, T'an Yen-k'ai, head of the political bureau, and several other members of these two executive sections of the Kuomingtang were present. In Hankow, Chiang would stand no chance against Borodin, supported by the peasant and labor unions; in Nanchang, Borodin would have equally little chance to oppose Chiang. Naturally the Wuhan group refused to accept Chiang's invitation. Thereupon Chiang went personally to Hankow to attempt persuasion. In this he failed, and withdrew precipitately to his stronghold. Whereupon Wuhan instituted a strong anti-Chiang movement. Chiang now called upon the Central Executive Committee to meet in Nanchang, in March, without the chaperonage of the Russians. Instead, on March 10, the left-wing members of the Committee assembled in Hankow, under the tutelage of the Russians. The center and right in general absented themselves. Practically speaking, the Wuhan junto was now Communist. Chiang was demoted from the post of commander-in-chief and chairman of the Standing Committee of the Central Executive Committee, the former post being superseded by a military commission, as announced by mandate of April 7 following. In the reorganized Standing Committee of the Executive Committee, Chiang was retained as a member, but Chang Chin-chiang, his friend, who had been acting for him as chairman, was dropped from membership. The new chairman was to be Wang Ching-wei, who was expected shortly to arrive. If Wuhan could have had its way at this time, T'ang Sheng-chih would have supplanted Chiang Kai-shek in the military leadership of the party; the latter was now merely the commander of the first nationalist army. For the nonce Borodin, the Communists, and the extreme left Kuomingtang were victorious. But Chiang, while almost out, was not down.

In an attempt to discredit Chiang and the right Kuomingtang generally, and with the powers in particular, and to consolidate their own position, Wuhan determined to seize Nanking and Shanghai, and institute an attack upon foreigners at the base of their "imperialistic" power. What was not clear at the time, but later became apparent, was that the foreigners and their interests in China were not so much the object of attack as they were the pawns in the game between right and left wings of the Kuomingtang, and the struggle between Chiang and Borodin. This is not, however, to minimize the important aspects of the old conflict still being waged under a new guise between Russia and Britain in Asia, and the new war between communism and capitalism.

To obtain control of southern and eastern Kiangsu, Chiang Kai-shek made use of anti-Communist forces under Generals Pai Ch'ung-hsi and Ho Ying-ch'in of Kwangsi. The troops of the first-named were the first Nationalists to enter the Chinese sections of Shanghai on March 22 (1927). This fact, in conjunction with the control of the foreign settlements of Shanghai by several thousand troops of the Western powers and Japan, prevented untoward incidents with respect to foreign residents such as had been envisaged by Wuhan, although there was serious fighting between labor unionists and Communists, and Nationalist troops in the Chinese-controlled sections of the city.

In Nanking developments were otherwise. Before Pai's and Ho's troops could reach this city, which was evacuated by Chang Tsung-ch'ang's northern armies on March 23, the Hunanese Communist-controlled troops of Ch'eng Ch'ien, a rival of Chiang who had been Sun Yat-sen's chief of military affairs in 1923, entered on the morning of the twenty-fourth and began a carefully planned and controlled attack on foreign residents, consulates, and other property, business and mission.

The looting and destruction of foreign property occurred for several days. Three British subjects, one American, one French, and one Italian were killed, and several others, including the British consul, were wounded. The Japanese consul, ill in bed, was shot at but not hit. A Chinese servant accompanying the American consul on his retreat to Socony Hill was killed. The Chinese civilians generally were unmolested, and many of them rendered heroic assistance to the imperiled foreigners. Many women and children had been

evacuated to Shanghai before Nanking fell to the Nationalists, but others had remained, believing either that
the city would not be taken or that foreigners, who in
general were sympathetic to the non-communistic revolutionists, would be in no danger. Of the women remaining, a considerable number were most disgracefully
treated. When all other efforts to protect foreign nationals had failed, and when it became evident that the
group besieged on Socony Hill could hold out no longer,
the American consul signaled for a barrage from the
foreign naval vessels lying in the river off their city.
British and American commanders at once responded,
and under cover of their fire the Socony Hill party
effected a dangerous withdrawal over the city wall to
the ships. The antiforeign attacks ceased almost in-
stantly, and the remaining foreigners were free to leave
the following day.[1]

Grossly exaggerated statements were made by the
Wuhan foreign minister, Mr. Eugene Ch'en, as to the
numbers of Chinese killed and wounded by the shells of
the foreign vessels. Since the area mainly fired upon was
open country, except for a few foreign residences, it is
clear that there could have been few casualties aside
from those suffered by the soldiers attacking Socony
Hill. Several members of rival looting bands killed and
injured each other. General Chiang Kai-shek later
stated that the probable casualties from the naval barrage were six killed and fifteen injured.

The policies of the Wuhan leaders, and the actions

---

[1] For an important account of the incidents mentioned see Mrs. Alice
Tisdale Hobart's *Within the Walls of Nanking*. London: Jonathan Cape,
1928.

sponsored by them, had a result exactly the opposite of what had been hoped. The powers did not intervene in the interior, and General Chiang found his position strengthened. Two days after the attack on Nanking he reached Shanghai, where he took steps to ally himself with the Shanghai bankers and merchants, and those earlier members of the Kuomingtang who had refused to co-operate with Borodin and the Communists. A successful attack upon the Communists and labor unions in the Shanghai area was immediately undertaken, and much blood was shed during the first two weeks of April. In compliance with Chiang's orders a similar purge of Communists and Russians took place at Canton on the night of the fifteenth of April.

T. V. Soong shortly arrived in Shanghai from Wuhan, as did Wang Ching-wei from Paris. Conferences of these men with Chiang Kai-shek, Hu Han-min, and others were held, and it was decided to call a meeting of the Central Executive Committee at Nanking for April 15. Before it could be assembled Wang Ching-wei, having failed to reconcile Chiang with Wuhan, retired to Hankow. Chiang's adherents proceeded to clear Nanking of Ch'eng Ch'ien's men and, supported by a Kuomingtang convention of his own, he established a government there on April 18 which disputed with that at Wuhan for leadership of the Nationalist movement. The latter continued to stand for radical, communistic internationalism; the former relied on nationalism and Dr. Sun's three people's principles. On April 17 Chiang was formally excommunicated from the Kuomingtang by the Wuhan group. He had committed the unpardonable sin of having, in the eyes of the Wuhan group, broken party discipline and acted for himself. This constituted him merely another militarist.

That the Chinese revolution was considered by Moscow as but a step toward world-revolution, and not an end in itself, was becoming more and more clear. Chang Tso-lin, the ruler of Peking and Manchuria, ordered a search of buildings adjacent to the Russian embassy in the legation quarter on April 6. The zeal of the raiders led them to search one of the buildings of the embassy itself. The documents found at this time proved beyond peradventure that Borodin was taking his orders from Moscow, and that the soviets were aiding Feng Yu-hsiang, as well as the southerners. Among the papers seized was a copy of a resolution recently passed in Moscow by the Executive Committee of the International Communist party, calling for the communization of China. This had reached Peking four days after the outbreak in Nanking. The seizure and search off Pukow, opposite Nanking, of the Russian steamer "Pamiat Lenina" on February 28–March 1, preceding; raids at Tientsin, on April 7, of Russian-controlled institutions; and the search of Arcos House, in London, on May 12, following, resulted in additional evidence with reference to the part being played by the soviets in China. This strengthened the position of Chiang Kai-shek and the less radical sections of the Kuomingtang.

The mandate promulgated by Wuhan on April 7 appointing (demoting) Chiang to the command of the Nationalist first army in the east, announced the appointment of Feng Yu-hsiang to the charge of the second Nationalist army. Feng had returned from Moscow, which he had reached on May 9, in October, 1926, and had at last decided that policy required definite adherence to the Kuomingtang. The split between Chiang and Borodin, in March and April, offered Feng an opportunity to play the one faction against the other. Nanking and Wuhan desired to destroy each other; at the same time each wanted to carry on the campaign against the northern war lords, Wu Pei-fu and Chang Tso-lin, and seize Peking. Success in this must result in tremendous prestige to the victor. In March the Feng-tien armies crossed the Yellow River and began their drive through Honan. Toward the end of the following month T'ang Sheng-chih's armies started northward from Hankow and, in May, Feng Yu-hsiang emerged from Shensi, by way of Tungkwan, along the Lunghai Railway. After severe fighting around Chumatien, between the twenty-first and the twenty-eighth of May, with heavy losses on both sides, Chang Tso-lin's forces had to retreat from Honan at the end of the month, and Feng took Chengchow. A week later he established his headquarters at Kaifeng. Yen Hsi-shan, the "peace lord" of Shansi, now (June 5) allied himself definitely with the Nationalists and raised their flag.

This campaign had important results. First of all, Feng ensconced himself in northeastern Honan, of which province he became defender—and controller. He was now in touch with Chiang Kai-shek, who had been campaigning simultaneously in northern Anhwei, and was able to play the rôle of arbiter between the Nationalist factions. To make clear his neutrality between them, he sent identical notifications of his successes in Honan to Nanking and to Wuhan. The Wuhan troops could now be recalled to Hankow where they were badly

needed to defend the government against imminent attacks of Chiang's adherents in Hunan to the south, and
of Yang Sen, an independent militarist from Szechwan,
who had earlier been an ally of Wu Pei-fu. By the middle of June the military menace to Wuhan had been
removed, at least temporarily.

A fortnight earlier (June 1), however, Messrs. Wang
Ching-wei and Sun Fo had received information of yet
another danger. A Hindu Communist observer in Wuhan, named Roy, who was a member of the Central Executive Committee of the Third International at Moscow, informed them that he and Borodin had received
instructions from that organization which had not been
shown to the left Kuomingtang members of the government. The new instructions outlined a program for (1)
the confiscation of land in Hupeh and Hunan by peasants acting through the Communist party without consultation with the Wuhan government; (2) for the immediate development within the Kuomingtang of Communist leadership (3) which should, in no long period,
effect the overthrow of the Kuomingtang itself; (4) for
the creation of a court to try counter-revolutionary militarists and punish them for obstructing the plans of the
Communist party; and (5) for the raising of an army of
twenty thousand Communists and fifty thousand peasants and laborers in Hupeh and Hunan.

To discuss their findings on this subject, as well as to
lay plans for the next military steps to be taken, the
Wuhan leaders—except Borodin, but including Blücher
—repaired to Chengchow where, during the second week
in June (1927), a conference was held with Feng Yu-
hsiang. The latter quickly learned that he had nothing

to expect in the way of munitions or funds from Wuhan,
and made it clear that he would not serve as a whip for
the chastisement of Chiang. It also became clear that if
Feng pursued Chang Tso-lin and expelled him from
Peking this would not strengthen either faction of the
Kuomingtang. On the subject of the growth of the
Russian-Communist power, and the spread of the
agrarian movement, there appeared a divergence of
opinion between the militarists and the civilians. The
former, especially T'ang Sheng-chih, were strongly inclined to carry out immediately a root-and-branch suppression of the peasants and laborers; the latter were less
aggressive, and advocated a milder policy of discourage-
ment of the working classes.

On the dissolution of the Chengchow conference Feng
proceeded to Hsuchow in Kiangsu, at the junction of
the Lunghai and Tientsin-Pukow railroads, where, from
June nineteenth to twenty-first, he conferred with
Chiang Kai-shek. Three days later he made an address
in which he declared that he would support Chiang with
an army of two hundred thousand men in the march to
Peking—where Chang Tso-lin, six days earlier, had
established his new government with himself as *tai-yuan-
shuai*, or generalissimo. Feng next sent a telegram to
Hankow demanding the dismissal of the Russians, the
suppression of the Communists and their agrarian and
social revolution, and the withdrawal from Wuhan of
certain of the Chinese leaders themselves. In the light
of the Chengchow conference, and the steps being taken
now in Hankow, it is apparent that this telegram was
sent as the result of an understanding with Wang Ching-
wei, Sun Fo, and their followers. A few days later

Chiang sent an ultimatum to Hankow making similar demands in a manner more blunt than Feng's.

Throughout June and the first two weeks of July the position of Borodin and the Communists was becoming untenable. The exposures of Russian-Communist influence, consequent upon the raids on the Russian embassy and consulates and other offices during the preceding months; the divulging of the instructions of the Third International by Roy; the opposition to the agrarian and labor movement manifested by the militarists of both Nanking and Wuhan; the enormous losses suffered by the Wuhan troops in the May campaign in Honan; Borodin's personal problems (Mme Borodin had been arrested on the "Pamiat Lenina" and was a prisoner in Peking) and the state of his health; and, most important of all, the conflicting instructions which he received from Moscow as a result of disagreement between the Trotsky and Stalin factions and the orders of the Third International—all combined to weaken Borodin's position and nullify his influence. He was caught between the conflicting forces in his own country and those in the country whose leaders he had come to advise. It is extremely doubtful whether he could have ultimately succeeded had there been unity of orders from Moscow; with disunity there, and a maelstrom of jealous leaders—civilian and military—mutually destructive theories and ambitions, and a growing antagonism to foreign interference of any sort, his position was hopeless.

On July 11, two days before the return of Wang Ching-wei and the other Wuhan leaders from the Chengchow conference, the first anti-Borodin demonstration took place outside the high adviser's office in Hankow. The return of the leaders was followed immediately by the holding of private meetings at which it was decided to break the alliance of the Kuomingtang with the Communist party, to outlaw the latter, to send Borodin and his Russian colleagues back to Russia, to suppress radicalism, to send a delegation to Moscow to make clear the position of the Kuomingtang, and to call a plenary session of the Central Executive Committee of the party for August 15.

On the eighteenth General Ho Chien put Hankow under martial law. He then banished Borodin, Blücher, and Eugene Chen to Kuling, a mountain resort not far away, arrested the Communist and labor leaders, and put many—four thousand, it was reported—to death. In the preceding May he had carried out a similar coup in Changsha, of which he was the Nationalist commander, against those who had been engaged in a reign of terror among the "anti-revolutionaries." The earlier practice had made him proficient in the suppression of radicals, as their colleagues now found in Hankow.

While forced to retire from China, Borodin was apparently not unwilling to leave. He realized that the wave of Russian-Communist influence had been broken on the rocks of Moscow's disunity, and China's new militarism, antiforeignism, and capitalistic conservatism. He had wrought well for Russia, but his day was done. On July 27 he and his entourage left Hankow by train on the first lap of the overland journey across Northwest China and Mongolia—all other routes of egress having been closed to him. At the railroad station various members of the government gathered to bid him farewell, among them Wang Ching-wei and T. V. Soong, the latter having returned to Hankow on July 12. Borodin's first stop was at Chengchow with Feng Yu-hsiang who, while anxious to have the Russians out of China and the social revolution squashed, was by no means ready to break with Moscow, which had for several years constituted his chief source of supplies.

With the withdrawal of Borodin, his chief Chinese adherents withdrew from Hankow. Mme Sun left for Shanghai, and shortly for Moscow, declaring that with the stoppage of the agrarian and social revolution, and the attacks being made on peasants and laborers, the revolution started by her husband had been betrayed, and that now there was nought but counter-revolution. In an impressive statement on the political situation issued in July she declared:

To guide us in the Chinese Revolution, Dr. Sun has given us his Three Principles and his three policies. It is the Third Principle, that of the livelihood of the people, that is at stake at the present time—the principle that answers the questions of fundamental social changes in China.

This Third Principle was felt by Dr. Sun to be basic in our Revolution. In this principle we find his analysis of social values and the place of the laboring and peasant classes defined. These classes become the basis of our strength in our struggle to overthrow imperialism, cancel the unequal treaties that enslave us, and effectively unify the country. These are the new pillars for the building of a new, free China. Without their support, the Kuomingtang, as a revolutionary party, becomes weak, chaotic and illogical in its social platform; without their support, political issues are vague. If we adopt any policy that weakens these supports, we shake the very foundation of our party, betray the masses and are falsely loyal to our leader. . . . .

Dr. Sun was poor. Not until he was fifteen years old did he have shoes for his feet, and he lived in a hilly region where it is not easy to be a barefoot boy. His family, until he and his brother were grown, lived almost from hand to mouth, in a hut. As a child he ate the cheapest food—not rice, for rice was too dear; his main nourishment was sweet potatoes.

Many times Dr. Sun has told me that it was in those days, as a poor son of a poor peasant family, that he became a revolutionary. He was determined that the lot of the Chinese peasant should not continue to be so wretched, that little boys in China should have shoes to wear and rice to eat. For this ideal he gave forty years of his life.

Yet to-day the lot of the Chinese peasant is even more wretched than in those days when Dr. Sun was driven by his great sense of human wrongs into a life of revolution. And to-day men, who profess to follow his banner, talk of classes and think in terms of a "revolution" that would virtually disregard the sufferings of those millions of poverty-stricken peasants of China.

To-day also we hear condemnation of the peasant and labor movement as a recent, alien product. This is false. Twenty, thirty years ago Dr. Sun was thinking and speaking in terms of a revolution that would change the status of the Chinese peasant. In his early twenties he wrote to Li Hung-chang, petitioning for social and economic reforms. In 1911 he wrote an article on the agrarian question in China, printed in Geneva, in *The Socialist*, in which he said that the basis of social and economic transformations in China is an agrarian revolution. . . . . I remember clearly the first All Kwangtung Peasants' Conference in Canton, in July, 1924. . . . . When he reached home he [Dr. Sun] said to me, "This is the beginning of the success of the revolution," and he told me again the part the oppressed people of China must play in their own salvation. . . . . Dr. Sun's policies are clear. If leaders of the party do not carry them out consistently then they are no longer Dr. Sun's true followers, and the party is no longer a revolutionary party, but merely a tool in the hands of this or that militarist. It will have ceased to be a living force working for the future welfare of the Chinese people, and will have become a machine, the agent of oppression, a parasite fattening on the present enslaving system. . . . . At the moment I feel that we are turning aside from Dr. Sun's policy of leading and strengthening the people; therefore I must withdraw until wiser policies prevail. . . . .[1]

The Wuhan Nationalist foreign minister, Eugene Ch'en, also left for Shanghai and Moscow. General

[1] Cf. Woo, *op. cit.*, Appendix II, pp. 270–73. Quoted by financial arrangement with Messrs. George Allen & Unwin, Ltd.

Blücher started overland from Hankow, in the wake of Borodin, on August 11. Teng Yen-ta, head of the propaganda section, was shortly proscribed and discreetly vanished. T'ang Sheng-chih, a militarist-opportunist of the old school, rather than a revolutionist, now attempted to set himself up in Hankow as *tuchun*-extraordinary of Hupeh and Hunan.

The publicly announced support of Chiang Kai-shek by Feng Yu-hsiang in June, and the collapse of Wuhan with the retirement of Borodin in July, did not place the Nanking leader in as fortunate a position as might have been expected. The landing of Japanese troops in Shantung, and their advance to Tsinan early in July, effectively blocked Chiang's and Feng's proposed move toward Peking. An attempt of Chiang to ally himself with Chang Tso-lin, in July, failed. The concentration of Chang Fa-k'uei's, Ch'eng Ch'ien's, and other pro-Communist troops at Kiukiang, followed by T'ang Sheng-chih's army, rendered it necessary for Chiang's forces to retreat southward toward Nanking, Chiang himself having earlier left the command in the north to Feng. The latter's troops, the Kuominchun, were defeated by those of Sun Ch'uan-fang and Chang Tsung-ch'ang, allies of Chang Tso-lin, when they attempted to cross from Honan to Shantung, and others were driven back along the Lunghai Railway from Hsuchow. From the military point of view, Chiang was in no condition to fight the up-river armies, and he was little stronger politically than he was militarily.

The logic of events called for a unification of the Kuomingtang, now that the Communists had been expelled and the Russians had withdrawn. But the old enmities between the ambitious Chinese leaders of the party rendered this difficult. Chiang disliked most, if not all, of the members of the left faction—especially Wang Ching-wei, who considered himself the natural leader of the party. Wang also had a private quarrel with Hu Han-min, who had had difficulties at times with Chiang as well—and was to have them again—and who felt that he, too, had a claim to the leadership of the party. The fact was that China had a plethora of leaders and a dearth of followers. As long as Chiang remained at Nanking it was impossible to heal the party breach. Accordingly, in the interests of civil and military unity, he suddenly resigned office on August 12 (1927) and withdrew to Shanghai, thence to his home in Chekiang, and somewhat later to Japan.

On retiring, Chiang denied being the cause of the split in the party, declared that he had no personal animus toward Borodin, although the latter had, he bluntly affirmed, been "hypocritical in his ways, trying to make the party serve as a scapegoat for his schemes." Nevertheless, he announced his approval of Sino-Russian cooperation. "Being a man of no scholarly attainments but fortunate enough to have been taught by Dr. Sun Yat-sen," Chiang stated, "I have made two resolutions which I will never abandon, namely (A) I acknowledge that the party is above everything and when the interests of the party are at stake each and every member of the party should follow the principles and the party without heeding his personal feelings and private interests. (B) I hold that the highest duty of a member of the party is to consolidate the foundation of the party at all costs, and for this reason I shall mobilise all available resources for the purpose of suppressing all who resort to clever ruses and hypocritical methods to shake the foundation of our party and pollute our party principles —in a word, all those who attempt to make the Kuomingtang a dead party without a soul."[1]

He ended with a threefold exhortation: that the Wuhan group should journey to Nanking and "jointly direct the future of our party," that the campaign for the capture of Peking should be continued, and that the authorities in Hunan, Hupeh, and Kiangsi should effect a thorough "cleansing" of the party of Communists.

Mid-August of 1927, therefore, witnessed the elimination, officially, of the two outstanding rivals of the period immediately following the death of Dr. Sun. It remained to be seen what the effect of the retirement of these outstanding personalities, and exponents of contradictory principles of revolution, would be. It was hardly to be expected that the forces, material and ideological, which they had headed could easily be reconciled, and such was shortly shown to be the case.

[1] Quoted by, and from, George E. Sokolsky, *The Kuomingtang*, chap. xxviii, in *The China Year Book* (1928), p. 1380.

CHAPTER IX

THE COMPLETION OF THE FIRST PHASE
OF THE NATIONALIST REVOLUTION

THE disintegration of the left Kuomingtang-Communist government at Hankow, and the withdrawal of Chiang Kai-shek from public life in August, 1927, were followed by a period of political confusion, business stagnation, and disillusionment, which bade fair for a time to end in a condition of affairs such as had prevailed through most of the country since the overthrow of the Manchus in 1911–12. The social and agrarian movements had been definitely interrupted; there was no unity of aim, or principle, among the revolutionary leaders, either civil or military; and the attempt to complete the formal unification of the country by the seizure of Peking had failed, partly as a result of Japanese intervention, but mainly on account of the strife within the party.

As minister of foreign affairs at Nanking, Chiang Kai-shek had appointed Mr. C. C. Wu. The latter became Nanking's chief negotiator in a conference at Kiukiang, on August 24, with the Hankow left leaders, Wang Ching-wei and Sun Fo, twelve days after Chiang's resignation. The Kiukiang conference was followed by a series of conferences at Shanghai, during the second week in September, and finally at Nanking in the middle of the month. These were participated in by all factions of the Kuomingtang, the Communists being excluded.

As a result of these conferences, and in the interim between party congresses, a Special Central Executive Committee and a Special Central Supervisory Committee were organized. These set up a new government at Nanking, on September 19, under the general supervision of T'an Yen-k'ai, with a bourgeois-capitalist orientation.

The conditions which prevailed were not conducive to the strengthening of the "September government," as it was called. Since it was not the creation of a party congress, it could not be considered as technically legitimate. Chiang Kai-shek, the outstanding general of the party, was in retirement. Mme Sun had broken with the party and started on a pilgrimage to Moscow. T'ang Sheng-chih was established independently in Hankow from which he was to be driven in October by two of Nanking's generals, only to be followed by one of them, Ch'eng Ch'ien, who in turn broke with Nanking on December 5 and set up independent rule. Feng Yu-hsiang was an unknown quantity biding his time. Yen Hsi-shan of Shansi was engaged in a renewed struggle with Chang Tso-lin's armies in the north. South China was in as great confusion as usual. Worst of all was the temporary failure of Wang Ching-wei and T. V. Soong to co-operate.

Wang withdrew from the Shanghai conferences on September 13, repaired to Kiukiang and Hankow for the nonce, and six weeks later appeared in Canton with Soong to set up a new Nationalist government which should be under civilian control and which would, of course, lean to the left. Here for several months the Kwangsi general, Li Chi-shen (Chai-sum), had been in authority, and had in April carried out the Russian and Communist purge in accordance with Chiang Kai-shek's instructions. Following the fall of the Wuhan government, Chang Fa-k'uei's army had split at Kiu-kiang; the Communist sections, under Generals Yeh Ting and Ho Lung, had moved southeastward to Swatow where they had established Red control; Chang Fa-k'wei, and the major part of the army, had reached Canton and nominally joined with Li, although actually the two generals were rivals for control of the city.

In mid-November, Wang Ching-wei and Li Chi-shen left Canton for Shanghai to attend a preparatory conference for the Fourth Plenary Session of the Central Executive Committee of the Kuomingtang.[1] Chang Fa-k'uei also left for Hongkong, supposedly to travel abroad. Arriving at Hongkong, Wang deserted Li, and secretly returned to Canton, as did Chang Fa-k'uei. Meanwhile, Chang's acting commander had seized control of the city, driving out Li Chi-shen's troops. Restored to power, Chang Fa-k'uei undertook to follow Li's policy of expelling the remaining Communists, including the remnants of the former strikers against Hongkong. While most of Chang's troops were pursuing Li's army into Kwangsi, a Communist coup in the city was carried out with the aid of Yeh Ting. This took place on December 11, and was accompanied by much destruction of property. Three days later General Li Fu-lin, a friend to Chiang Kai-shek, carried out an anti-Communist coup, broke the power of the Reds, and put many of them to death.

The anti-Communist coup was accompanied by an

[1] Cf. Arnold J. Toynbee (ed.), *Survey of International Affairs*, 1927, pp 360–61.

attack upon the Russian consulate-general. The entire staff was arrested and subjected to public humiliation and insult, several members being summarily put to death. The consulate was closed, and the consul-general and the surviving members of his staff were later deported.

Simultaneously the Russian consulates at Shanghai and Hankow were closed and their staffs deported. In Hankow, but not at Shanghai, there was much brutality directed against both Russian and Chinese Communists connected with the closing of the consulate. Many were imprisoned and several Chinese were executed. All Russian consulates in Central and Southern China were now ordered closed by Nanking.

The year 1927, which had opened with the Russians in practically dictatorial control of a large part of the country, ended with their official elimination south of the Yangtze and strained relations with the soviet government of Moscow. Russian and Chinese Communist influences were, however, by no means broken, as subsequent events were to prove; they were merely driven underground.

The withdrawal of Chiang Kai-shek had not resulted in the establishment of a strong government at Nanking for the reasons stated. On November 10 he returned to Shanghai from Japan where he had gone, according to statements made at the time, to obtain the consent of the Soong family to his marriage to Miss Soong Mei-ling, a sister of Mme Sun Yat-sen, Mme. H. H. Kung, and T. V. Soong. Chiang's former wife, according to Russian reports,[1] had kept Wuhan supplied with news

---

[1] Cf. Fischer, *op. cit.*, II, 667.

of her husband's movements following his break with
Wuhan in the preceding March and April. Instead of
committing suicide, as, according to the same source, he
at one time contemplated, he broke with his wife, and
supplanted her by one more devoted to his cause. The
marriage with Miss Soong took place in Shanghai on
December 1 (1927).

Chiang and Wang Ching-wei had for some time been
drawing together on the basis of a common opposition
to the September government at Nanking. On November 4, six days before Chiang's return, Wang had sent a
telegram from the south expressing unalterable opposition to the Special Committee at Nanking on the ground
that it was a counter-revolutionary organization and
that it constituted "an obstacle to the convention of the
4th plenary session of the Central Executive and Supervisory Committees."[1] Chiang now headed a center
group in the Kuomingtang which stood for conciliation
of the Western Hills, the Kwangsi, and the left-wing
groups, and presided over conferences held in his residence in the French concession at Shanghai during the
week preceding his marriage. Wang supported Chiang,
while Li Chi-shen held conferences at his Shanghai residence at which Wang's military supporters in the south
were bitterly denounced, especially Chang Fa-kwei.
The Communist attack on Canton, on December 14,
greatly strengthened Chiang and his center group.

On December 10 Chiang was offered his former post of
commander-in-chief, which he indicated his readiness
to accept. Early in January, 1928, he returned to Nanking where he completely dominated the situation. On

[1] *The China Year Book* (1929–30), p. 1164.

the first of the following month the Fourth Plenary Session of the Central Executive and Central Supervisory committees of the Kuomingtang was opened in Nanking, and a reorganization of the party, as well as of the government, was entered upon. Chiang was officially restored to office as commander-in-chief, and, in addition, was made chairman of the Central Executive Committee and of the Military Council. The holding of these positions by one man meant the postponement for an indefinite period of the application of the principle of civilian control of the Kuomingtang for which Wuhan, and especially Wang Ching-wei, had stood. The union with the soviets and the Chinese Communists was definitely broken; the *San Min* principles of Dr. Sun were reaffirmed, and it was made clear that the Nationalist revolution had for its object the salvation and the domination of no particular social group. The labor and peasant groups were now further discouraged. All this meant victory for the "bourgeois-capitalists."

Having failed in principle at Wuhan, Canton, Shanghai, and Nanking, Wang Ching-wei had again withdrawn into European exile before the convening of the Fourth Plenary Session on February 1. Messrs. Hu Han-min, C. C. Wu, and Sun Fo now decided to follow his example and travel abroad for a period.

Mr. Wu was succeeded as foreign minister until May by General Huang Fu, one of the early Tung Meng Hui–Kuomingtang revolutionists of the 1911–13 period. He was followed in office in June by Mr. C. T. Wang, who has continued to hold the portfolio of foreign affairs to the present (August, 1931), and who has been remarkably successful in negotiating new treaties with the powers.[1] Both these ministers were born in Chekiang, General Chiang's home province. Mr. T. V. Soong, now the commander-in-chief's brother-in-law, assumed the duties of minister of finance, perhaps the most difficult post in the government, and has acquitted himself so well that he has at times been spoken of as the Alexander Hamilton of the revolution.

The manifesto of the Fourth Plenary Session announced that the Nationalist revolution had "entered the period of political and economic reconstruction" and would thereafter "devote itself to the strengthening of its foundation by carefully carrying out the instructions of its late leader and exerting to the utmost of its ability in completing various programmes of reconstruction," as laid down in Dr. Sun's *Principles of National Reconstruction*.

On the councils and committees were appointed most of the outstanding men who had at one time or another been connected with the party, regardless of faction, and of their presence in, or absence from, the country. Men of such divergent views as the conservative Wang Chung-hui; Chang Chi of the Western Hills group; the elder statesman Tsai Yuan-pei, sometime chancellor of the Peking National University, and an "intellectual anarchist"; Feng Yu-hsiang of the Kuominchun; Yen Hsi-shan of Shansi; T'an Yen-k'ai of the Wuhan and Nanking September governments; Li Tsung-jen and Li Chi-shen of the Kwangsi faction; the exile, Wang Ching-wei, of the extreme radical left; and Sun Fo, Hu Han-

[1] Cf. H. B. Morse and H. F. MacNair, *Far Eastern International Relations*, chap. xxx. Boston: Houghton Mifflin, 1931.

min, and C. C. Wu of the right, who had gone abroad
before the session was convened, were made members of
the Government Council of forty-nine members.[1]

The immediate object of such a high degree of superficial unity was the reopening of the campaign against
Chang Tso-lin, Chang Tsung-ch'ang, and Sun Ch'uang-
fang, the surviving war-lord opponents of the Kuomingtang in the north. For this campaign Chiang Kai-shek
resumed command of the first-army group, while Feng
Yu-hsiang and Yen Hsi-shan commanded the second-
and third-army groups, respectively. Later Li Tsung-
jen was appointed to command the fourth-army group.
It was broadly agreed that Chiang's forces should push
north on both sides of the Tientsin-Pukow Railway;
Feng's troops would do the same along the Peking-Han-
kow line; while Yen's men would attack the area west
of Peking and along the Peking-Suiyuan line. On April 7
the campaign was opened; by the thirtieth part of
Chiang's troops had reached Tsinan, the capital of
Shantung.

In the preceding year Japan's intervention in Shantung had been a contributing factor to the failure of the
Nationalists to capture Peking. On April 20, 1928, the
Japanese legation in Peking notified the Foreign Office
of the *Tai-yuan-shuai* of the intention of Tokyo to dis-
patch some five thousand men "by way of Tsingtao to
places along the Kiaochow-Tsinan Railway for the purpose of protecting the Japanese residents, and as an
emergency measure, in view of the growing seriousness
of the situation there, pending their arrival, to send to

[1] Cf. G. E. Sokolsky, "The Kuomingtang," *The China Year Book* (1929–
30), chap. xxvi, p. 1173.

Tsinan three companies out of the Japanese Infantry stationed in China."[1] Despite Peking's protests, and acceptance of the responsibility for the protection of Japanese and lives and property, the troops were sent. When Chiang Kai-shek reached Tsinan on May 1, he found them in control of most of the foreign part of the city, and of the Kiaochow Railway which links it with Tsingtao. On April 28 Nationalist troops had cut this line just east of Tsinan, despite a warning from the Japanese commander, Fukuda, that it must not be touched.

At first it appeared that conflict between the Chinese and the Japanese armies might be avoided, but on May 3 serious fighting between them occurred which was renewed May 8–10. Considerable losses of life and destruction of property ensued. The Chinese were defeated, and the Japanese assumed control of the Kiaochow Railway, part of the Tientsin-Pukow line immediately north and south of Tsinan, and of that city itself.

The Tsinan incident prevented Chiang from participating directly in the continued advance to Peking. He appointed a deputy commander of his army group, which was shortly placed under the command of Feng Yu-hsiang, withdrew westward to plan the forward movements of the other Nationalist armies, and shortly returned to Nanking. There he appointed Yen Hsi-shan to the command of the Peking and Tientsin gendarmerie—in this way preventing Feng from enjoying a victory which had been denied to himself, and keeping the latter, for the time being, from becoming a source of

[1] *The China Year Book* (1929–30), p. 879.

danger in the north at the moment of Chang Tso-lin's passing.

Realizing that the intervention of Japan in Shantung was not to result as it had in the previous year, and that his own position was weakened by it, and receiving from the Japanese minister in Peking an exceedingly plain warning, on May 18, of the desirability of his immediate withdrawal to Mukden, Chang Tso-lin retired from Peking on the night of June 2–3. On the fourth his train was bombed as it was drawing into Mukden, and Chang himself was mortally wounded, if not killed; his death was officially announced on the twenty-first. His eldest son, Hsueh-liang, had assumed supreme command of Manchuria on the preceding day.

On June 8, five days after Chang Tso-lin's withdrawal from the northern capital Yen Hsi-shan's troops marched into that city, followed by Yen himself, accompanied by Pai Ch'ung-hsi, the Kwangsi leader from Wuchang, two or three days later. The main campaign was now at an end. Officially, but only in theory, all of China proper was under the control of the Nationalist government at Nanking. The object of the campaign having been accomplished, Chiang, on June 10, officially laid down his powers as commander-in-chief and chairman of the Military Council which he had assumed four months before. Eleven days later Nanking hopefully changed the name of Peking, that is, "northern capital," to P'eiping, "northern peace." Nanking was now declared to be the capital of the country.

Shortly, there occurred a ceremony reminiscent of that which Dr. Sun had carried out before the tomb of the first Ming emperor at Nanking in 1912. On July 3

Chiang Kai-shek reached Peking, to be followed there by Feng Yu-hsiang three days later; other government and military leaders had also arrived. At Pi Yün-ssu, a magnificent Buddhist temple in the Western Hills, Sun Yat-sen's body was lying waiting final sepulture at Nanking. To his temporary tomb the Nationalist leaders resorted on July 6 to announce to the spirit of Dr. Sun the fulfilment of his wishes—the fall of the northern war lords, the capture of Peking, and the unification of the country under a government based on his principles. That the widow and the only son of the leader were in exile because they did not approve of the interpretation for the moment of his principles, and that Chang Tsung-ch'ang and his troops were still causing confusion in northeastern Chihli, appear not to have been notified to his spirit.

CHAPTER X

THE FIVE-POWER GOVERNMENT
AT NANKING

THE capture of Peking, which was considered to complete the official unification of the country, was interpreted as ending the first of the three phases—the military and destructive phase—of the revolution outlined by Dr. Sun. Although fighting in the north, particularly in Shantung, continued through the remainder of the year, and on into 1929, the Nanking leaders entered with enthusiasm upon the consolidation of the position of their government. In this they were supported by the Chinese business groups in Shanghai who participated in an economic conference, under the lead of Mr. T. V. Soong, during the latter part of June (1928). Army disbandment, to be followed by colonization by the soldiers, reorganization of the currency and the establishment of a single national mint, the budgeting of government funds and the cutting-down of expenditures—all these were advocated by this conference. Military and financial conferences followed in Nanking in July. Here the old rivalries between jealous, suspicious, and ambitious generals, and the age-old struggle between the principles of centralization of the government and autonomy for the provinces, prevented any practicable sulution being found for the manifold problems faced by the government. Symptomatic of both these difficulties was the increasing strain through-

out the year 1928 in the relations between General
Chiang Kai-shek and the Kwangsi faction.

With the greatest difficulty Chiang finally convened
the Fifth Plenary Session of the Central Executive Committee of the Kuomingtang on August 8 (1928). It
should have been opened a week earlier but disagree-
ments between the Kwangsi faction and its supporters,
and the left wing, prevented it. The session broke up
within a week of its opening as the result mainly of a
dispute regarding the proposed abolition of the party
branch political councils in the provinces. The left-wing
leaders opposed, while the Kwangsi group favored, their
retention.

A somewhat passive, but disturbing, participant was
Marshal Feng Yu-hsiang, who played the dual rôle of
Diogenes and Cato: "He scandalized official etiquette
by driving about the city in a motor lorry dressed in a
common soldier's uniform and a shocking old hat, and
lectured the Kuomingtang on extravagant living and
the lavishness with which rewards were served out but
no punishments. . . . ."[1] Having surveyed the political
and financial leanness of Nanking, he withdrew to his
own satrapy of Shensi and Kansu. Here he entered upon
the extirpation of Chinese Moslem insurgents against
his rule who appear to have been stimulated by Chang
Tso-lin in the preceding spring as part of his campaign
against the Kuominchun. Within six weeks Feng had the
Moslems retreating—but slaughtering the Chinese infi-
dels whom they could reach. Famine played a part in
the grim struggle. It is estimated that between a quarter
and a half million lives were sacrificed as a result of war

[1] *North China Herald*, CLXX, No. 3204 (January 5, 1929), 7.

and famine in the northwest. But, for the moment, Chiang Kai-shek and Nanking were safe from attack by Feng.[1] This gave them a chance to concentrate upon the Kwangsi generals in the following year, when it became evident that the military phase of the revolution had been completed only in theory and aspiration by the fall of Peking and the promulgation in October of an Organic Law of the National Government of the Republic of China.

This Law was one of the two outstanding results of the August session of the Central Executive Committee; the other was the fruitless, but nevertheless statesmanlike, memorandum of Minister Soong demanding the putting into effect by the government of a budget system. Mr. Soong declared that he had been forced to find $1,600,000 silver every five days throughout the period of the recent campaign for Peking, although he had had no control of appropriations or expenditures.[2] Despite the obvious need for a budgeting of national finances, no provision looking toward such was made until late in 1930.

Dr. Sun had called for the promulgation of a provisional—not a permanent—constitution to serve as a guard for the rights of the government and of the people during the second, or tutelage, phase of the revolution. Something of this nature the Nanking Law Codification Bureau demanded should now be prepared, and the Plenary Session of the Central Executive Committee approved the idea before its dissolution on mid-August.

---

[1] Arnold J. Toynbee (ed.), *Survey of International Affairs*, 1928, p. 385.

[2] *North China Herald*, CLXX, No. 3204 (January 5, 1929), 7; *The China Year Book* (1929–30), p. 635.

Messrs. Tai Chi-t'ao, a Szechwanese who had served as secretary to Dr. Sun in 1913 during his exile in Japan; Wang Ch'ung-hui, Dr. Sun's outstanding friend in the legal profession; and Hu Han-min quickly prepared the document known as the Organic Law. Hu had returned to China early in September and, after some hesitation, had happily expressed his approval of the Nanking régime, a fact of considerable significance in the stabilization of the government. The Organic Law was prepared between September 19 and October 3, and was formally instituted on October 4.

On the day on which the Organic Law was completed the Central Executive Committee of the party promulgated a set of six principles "with a view to carrying out Dr. Sun's *Three Principles of the People* in accordance with the *Outline of National Reconstruction* and with a view to training the people during the Period of Tutelage in the exercise of political authority until the Constitutional Period begins in order to arrive at a democracy of all the people. . . . ." The six principles provided for the guidance of the people by the Kuomingtang National Congress "on behalf of the People's Convention"; for the execution of the will of the Congress by the Central Executive Committee; for the training of the people "in the gradual adoption of the four political powers, namely: election, recall, initiative, and referendum . . . ."; for the wielding of power by the national government through the five divisions outlined in the Organic Law; for the supervision and guidance of the national government by the "Political Council of the Central Executive Committee of the Kuomingtang of China"; for the "amendment and interpretation of the

Organic Law . . . . by resolutions adopted by the Political Council of the Central Executive Committee of the Kuomingtang."

Of outstanding significance was the specific declaration in the preamble to the Organic Law of October 4 that it was ordained and promulgated by the Kuomingtang. In other words, China was to continue to be ruled for an indefinite period—until the second phase of the revolution should end—by a *party*. No provision was made for legal opposition to the established government. In this the revolutionary leaders followed the precedents established by the Russian bolshevists and the Italian fascists.

The Organic Law is in six chapters, exclusive of the preamble. It contains no bill of rights.[1] Chapter i provides that the "National Government shall exercise all the governing powers of the Republic of China," including the supreme command of all forces, the right to declare and end war, to grant amnesties, and to restore civic rights. It outlines a government composed of five Yuan, or boards, namely, the executive, legislative, judicial, examination, and control, whose presidents and vice-presidents shall be "appointed from among the State Councillors." These last number twelve to sixteen, and constitute a council which conducts national affairs and settles points referred to them by two or more of the Yuans. Provision is made for a "President [or Chairman] of the National Government"—not a president of China—who receives foreign diplomats, represents the government in state functions, concurrently serves as commander-in-chief of the forces of the re-

[1] Cf. *The China Year Book* (1929-30), pp. 709-12.

public, presides over the State Council, and signs all laws and mandates issued by that group. But these must be countersigned by the presidents of the five Yuan.

Chapters ii, iii, iv, v, and vi of the Organic Law outline the powers of the five Yuan. The executive Yuan, which was presided over by T'an Yen-k'ai until his death in 1929, is declared to be "the highest executive organ of the National Government"; it has a president and vice-president, and its duties are carried out through a non-stated number of ministers and commissions which latter take charge of specified executive matters. The ministries are headed by a minister and a political and an administrative vice-minister; the last is a routine officer less powerful than his political colleague. Each commission has a chairman and a vice-chairman. The ministers and vice-ministers, chairmen and vice-chairmen, are appointed and removed by the president of the Yuan. The ministers and the commission chairmen may, on occasion, attend meetings of the State Council and of the legislative Yuan. Into the latter the executive Yuan may introduce bills within its competence, budgets, recommendations for amnesties, and matters having to do with war, peace, and international affairs. Other matters loosely defined, or entirely undefined, may be settled by the executive Yuan itself.

The legislative Yuan, under the presidency of Hu Han-min until his resignation on March 1, 1931, is the "highest legislative organ of the National Government." It is composed of "from forty-nine to ninety-nine members, who shall be appointed by the National Government at the instance of the President of the said Yuan."

The term of office for its members is two years, and they may not be concurrently "non-political administrative officials of the various organs of the central or local governments." The resolutions of the legislative Yuan "shall be decided upon and promulgated by the State Council."

The judicial Yuan, under the presidency of Wang Ch'ung-hui, is the "highest judicial organ of the National Government," and takes charge of "judicial trials, judicial administration, disciplinary punishment of officials, and trial of administrative cases. The granting of pardons and reprieves and the restitution of civic rights shall be submitted by the President of the Judicial Yuan to the National Government for approval and action." This Yuan may "introduce in the legislative Yuan bills on matters within its own competence."

Of outstanding interest to foreign students of the Chinese revolution, are the examination and the control Yuan, which are peculiarly Chinese, and constitute a *liaison* between old and new Chinese governmental concepts. In 1905 the ancient system of literary examinations which had served as the road trodden by aspirants to the civil service was swept away by the old empress dowager, Tzǔ Hsi.[1] Reform of the system, rather than abolition, would, in the light of subsequent developments, appear to have been the wiser move. Dr. Sun and his posthumous followers, realizing the need for some system of examination of knowledge and general qualifications of would-be officials, outlined such in the examination Yuan, over which Tai Chi-t'ao was to pre-

[1] Cf. *supra*, chap. i, p. 12.

side. "All public functionaries shall be appointed only after having, according to law, passed an examination and their qualifications for public service having been determined by the examination Yuan." Not being retroactive, this provision would not, of course, affect those already in office; if, and as, it is applied to later candidates it should go far toward building up a qualified civil service. The examination Yuan may also "introduce in the legislative Yuan bills on matters within its own competence." No provision was incorporated with reference to the size of the Yuan.

The control Yuan, the presidency of which was offered to Ts'ai Yuan-p'ei, who declined it, and later given to Yu Yu-jen of Shensi, is the "highest supervisory organ" of the government, and controls impeachment and auditing. It is composed of "from nineteen to twenty-nine members, who shall be appointed by the National Government at the instance of the President of the said Yuan." The security of their term of office is to be determined by law, and the members may not "concurrently hold any office in any of the organs of the central or local governments." This Yuan, like the others, also has the right to "introduce in the legislative Yuan bills on matters within its own competence."

The incorporation of the control Yuan, provision for the inauguration of which was not made until late in 1930,[1] means the restoration in essence of the principle of the ancient imperial censorate which is to be traced to the third century before Christ.[2] Originally serving

[1] Cf. *post*, chap. xi, pp. 180–81.

[2] Cf. P. C. Hsieh, *The Government of China (1644–1911)*, pp. 87–98; S. Couling (ed.), *Encyclopaedia Sinica*, p. 85; H. B. Morse, *Trade and Administration of China* (3d ed.), p. 45.

as critics of the emperor, the censors' duties were broadened to include criticism of the officials. The censors were generally known as the "eyes and ears officials." Their position was honorable and influential, but onerous and not without personal danger to the holder. According to Wang Ch'ung-hui, who had often discussed the principles of the five-power constitution with Dr. Sun, the practical application of the principles of the censorate caused much cogitation on the part of the latter.

No attempt was made in 1928 to work out the details of application of the censorate principle, or any other, involved in the Organic Law. The main object was to agree upon working principles and to leave details to be agreed upon as occasion should arise, after the government should have consolidated its position. The power and the duty of interpretation and amendment of the basic law were, by separate resolution, left to the Central Executive Committee of the Kuomingtang.[1]

Co-operating with the State Council and the five Yuan provided by the Organic Law are the Central Military Council and the Central Research Council which were not mentioned in that Law. Through the former, in time of war, the chairman of the State Council functions as commander-in-chief of all forces of the republic. At other times the Military Council is controlled by the minister of war.

The Research Council, which carries out its duties through several bureaus, heads all scientific and academic research on behalf of the central government, and

[1] Cf. Mr. Wang's article on the preparation of the law in the *China Critic*, October 25, 1929, quoted in *The China Year Book* (1929–30), pp. 1186–88.

is presided over by a director appointed by the government.

As specified in the preamble to the Organic Law of October 4, 1928, the "national government," as it has been termed since that date, is the creature of the Kuomingtang. There is no pretense that sovereignty at present rests in the people; on the contrary, it is considered to lie in the Party Congress. China is ruled, in so far as the Nanking government is concerned, by the Kuomingtang, which, in 1929, had a registered membership of about 422,000, of whom more than one-ninth were overseas Chinese. This means, therefore, that about one Chinese in one thousand is a member of the party in power, and no opposition party may legally exist.

To understand the relationship between the government and the party it is necessary to consider the organization of the Kuomingtang. The constitution of the latter was adopted at the First National Congress in 1924.[1] Amended by the second and third congresses of 1926 and 1929, respectively, it is the basic law of the Chinese constitution.

Technically, the supreme organ of the Kuomingtang is the Biennial Congress, which is composed of members elected in theory—until March 27, 1929—by the provincial, special municipal, and special administrative district conventions.[2] The Congress may, under certain conditions, be convened oftener than every two years, or it may be postponed for not longer than one year. Its duties are fourfold: (1) to approve the reports of the government; (2) to amend the constitution of the party;

[1] Cf. *supra*, chap. vii, p. 93.   [2] Cf. *post*, chap. xi, p. 165.

(3) to enunciate new aims for the government; (4) to elect the members of the Central Executive Committee of the party, and the Central Supervisory Committee.

The Central Executive Committee is supposed to have thirty-six members who meet in plenary session at least semiannually. The official duties of this Committee are: "(1) To represent the Party in external relations; (2) To carry out the resolutions of the National Congress; (3) To organize Party headquarters in different provinces and districts; (4) To organize Central Party headquarters; (5) To decide on the allocations of the Party contributions and finances."[1] As mentioned above, the Central Executive Committee has the duty, also, of interpreting the Organic Law of October 4, 1928.

The Central Supervisory Committee likewise meets at least semiannually; it has twelve members whose duties are: "(1) To decide on the punishment of members violating the Party discipline; (2) To audit the accounts of the Central Executive Committee; (3) To review the progress of Party affairs; (4) To supervise the conduct of the National Government and see if its policies and record conform to the policies of the Party."[2] When not in session each of these committees is represented by a Standing Committee of from five to nine members elected from and by the Committee. That of the Central Executive Committee holds supreme power when neither the Committee nor the Congress is in session.

To the Central Political Council of the party the Central Executive Committee delegates considerable ad-

[1] M. T. Z. Tyau, *Two Years of Nationalist China*, pp. 26–27. Shanghai: Kelly and Walsh, 1930.

[2] *Ibid.*

ministrative power, but retains the right of approval or disapproval. This council earlier had a membership of from forty-nine to ninety-nine members; included in it were all the members of the Central Executive Committee itself and the State Council of the national government. By a resolution of the Central Executive Committee, however, following the Third Party Congress of March, 1929, the membership was cut to 50 per cent, or less, of the combined membership of the Central Executive and Supervisory committees to be chosen by the Standing Committee of the former.

The Central Political Council meets weekly and refers its resolutions to the State Council which, meeting weekly, passes most of them on to the executive Yuan; this, in turn, refers them to the appropriate ministry or commission. By the Central Political Council of the party the presidents and vice-presidents of the governmental Yuan are appointed from the membership of the State Council.

During the session of the Fourth Plenary Session of the Central Executive Committee, in November, 1930, it was decided that a closer linking of the Central Political Council with the executive departments of the government was desirable, and that it should be made by the appointment of the political vice-ministers as special secretaries of the political council committees on foreign affairs, military affairs, finance, economics, education, legislation, and district autonomy. By a decision of the Standing Committee of the Central Executive Committee on November 25 (1930), "Persons shouldering high responsibilities of the Party and the State and whose official status are above the rank of *Teh-jen* (1st

rank specially appointed) may, upon the decision of the
Central Executive Committee, be appointed Members
of the Central Political Council. The number of such
members shall not, however, exceed one-fourth of the
membership of the Council (who are members of the
Central Committees)."

While the power of legislative initiative lies in theory
with the national government through the legislative
Yuan, the actual control of legislation is in the party.
After the legislative Yuan has passed a measure, it must
be referred to the State Council, which passes it on to
the Central Executive Committee by way of the Central
Political Council, or directly to the Central Executive
Committee which passes it in turn to the Central Political Council. When approved by both the Central
Executive Committee and the Central Political Council,
the measure is then returned to the State Council for
promulgation.

From time to time the presidents and vice-presidents
of the five Yuan, the chairmen of the executive commissions, and the ministers of state under the executive
Yuan (that is, the ministers of the interior and health;
foreign affairs; military affairs; the navy; finance; agriculture, mining, industry, commerce, and labor; education; communications; and railways) meet in governmental administrative conference for purposes of co-
ordination of their respective functions. Likewise the
members of the State Council, the presidents of the five
Yuan, and others elected by the National Conference
meet in governmental conference, under the presidency
of the chairman of the State Council, to consider and
enunciate government policies, and to see that the latter

coincide with those of the party. The National Conference, just mentioned, is representative of the party, and is composed of the members of the Central Executive and Central Supervisory committees. This Conference lays down the broad principles of both party and government concerning domestic and foreign affairs.

Reference has been made to the dispute which developed during the Fifth Plenary Session of the Central Executive Committee at Nanking in August, 1928. This arose indirectly out of the provisions in chapter ii of the constitution of the Kuomingtang for the establishment within the provinces, and subdivisions of the provinces, of a duplication of the party machinery. According to the party constitution, the unit of the Kuomingtang is the local, or subprecinct, committee, known in the vernacular as the *tangpu*. This unit is composed of a minimum of five members. Above it are the subdistrict, the district (or Hsien), and the province, in each of which there are a party convention and executive and supervisory committees. As at Nanking, the executive and supervisory committees of the province, the district, and the subdistrict elect their standing committees.

By chapter iii of the party constitution provision is made for a practically parallel organizational development in special administrative areas, such as Tibet and Mongolia; in cities having special administrative organizations; and in areas outside China in which numbers of Chinese reside.

The briefest analysis of the Nationalist party and the national government makes clear certain factors and characteristics of importance. In the first place, it is clear that the two organizations are inextricably inter-

twined in organs which are based primarily on Russian
soviet ideology. This is to be traced to the early Borodin period of 1924–25. The Organic Law of 1928 added
the earlier ideas of Dr. Sun for a system which should
be based on Chinese as well as Western European
thought and experience. To the division of governmental powers along executive, legislative, and judicial lines
he had added the two Chinese divisions of the civil
service and the censorate, thereby evolving a system
more in keeping with Chinese experience than either the
parliamentary or presidential or soviet systems of the
West. Of his plans for a five-power constitution Dr. Sun
was exceedingly proud, describing it as "the fruit
exclusively of my work," and "the fruit of my labours
alone."[1] It was characteristic of the strife between the
party factions that while the ideas of the party founder,
or *tsung-li*, as Dr. Sun came to be called, were incorporated in the Organic Law, no real swing away from
the committee system of the soviets resulted; jealousy,
and fear of power centered in one man, prevented this.

The necessity of the moment resulted, nevertheless, in
the provision for a president (or chairman) of the national government, who is also officially commander-in-
chief of all armed forces in the "republic." Supreme
power does not lie in the government, however, but in
the Standing Committee of the Central Executive Committee of the Kuomingtang which interprets and amends
the Organic Law. The chairman of the Standing and
Central committees is the president of the national government, and commander-in-chief, who is in reality the

---

[1] Cf. *Memoirs of a Chinese Revolutionary*, Appendix II, p. 239. Quoted by
courtesy of Hutchinson & Co. (publishers), London.

ruler of that part of China which accepts the mandates of Nanking.

The interlocking of party and government committees, in powers and in personnel, provides a constant check by the former upon the latter. Without the approval of the Kuomingtang the national government can do nothing. The members of the Standing Committee of the party Central Executive Committee are outside and above all law, organic and other. There is no check upon them, and from their decisions as a group there is no recourse, except passive or military resistance outside the immediate sphere of Nanking's influence. This accounts for the arbitrary actions of the government which have occurred from time to time—for example, the practical confiscation of valuable land and shop-frontage from otherwise poor owners in and outside the capital for the building of the road to Sun Yat-sen's tomb on Purple Mountain—and which have caused bitter criticism by those, such as Hu Shih, the noted intellectual, who have dared to voice complaint.

Since 1928 the civilian element has been, in theory, superior to the military in both government and party. Inasmuch as the offices of chairman of the Central Executive Committee and its Standing Committee, the presidency of the national government and the State Council, and that of the Military Council are concurrently held by General Chiang Kai-shek, no comments upon the practical relationship of the civil and military elements within the party and the government appear necessary.

In outlining his ideas for the revolutionary reorgan

ization of the country[1] Dr. Sun discussed the development of local government in the county, or *hsien*, which
should become "a true self-governing unit" which could
"count on the revolutionary government taking up a
favourable attitude toward it, and granting it all its
constitutional rights under the provisional constitution." In attempting to provide for the construction of
a government from the base to the apex, Dr. Sun was
in accord with the ideals of political scientists; probably,
also, he hoped to bridge the gap generally existent in
China between the central and the local administrative
units. To the present, however, the forces of particular-
ism, provincialism, and sectionalism have been too
strong for the practical application of the idealism of
the party founder. These have manifested themselves
through two channels mainly: the provincial, or super-
provincial, branch political councils, and the locals or
tangpus. In many cases the controlling members of
these two groups have either directly or indirectly appointed themselves to office, and have merely theoretically taken orders from Nanking. The *tangpus* have
been a constant source of irritation to the government,
to the people, and to foreigners resident in China. Little
groups, often composed mainly of self-willed, self-
styled patriots, they have interfered with business, educational, and other institutions without bothering generally to refer matters to the larger units of the local
government or to follow the will of the capital when the
latter has made known its wishes.

More dangerous to the government on occasion have
been the branch political councils at Canton, Hankow,

[1] Cf. *ibid.*, chap. iv, pp. 120–21.

Kaifeng, Taiyuan, Peking, and Mukden. When the re-organized Nanking government was formally instituted on October 10, 1928, and Chiang Kai-shek assumed an all-embracing presidency, the relation of the government and the party to the branch councils was not clearly defined. Yen Hsi-shan, momentarily minister of the interior and a state councilor, was in control of the Branch Council in his capital, Taiyuan, in Shansi; over the one established after the fall of Peking he came to have partial control. When a council was formed at Mukden, it was the creature of Chang Hsueh-liang who controlled Manchuria and who was also a member of the State Council of the new Nanking government. Feng Yu-hsiang, who was appointed to membership in the same as well as minister of war, headed the Branch Council in Kaifeng. These three generals, of somewhat uncertain loyalty, ruled North China—except parts of Shantung where the Japanese were still in control—including Manchuria. The state councilor, Li Tsung-jen of the Kwangsi faction, controlled Central China and the Branch Council at Hankow, while Li Chi-shen, another Kwangsi general, ruled Canton and the Branch Council there. Supposed, constitutionally, to work closely with the central government, these regional councils, and their controllers, in reality consulted their own interests and were centrifugal, rather than centripetal, agencies. This was to be demonstrated a short six months later.

Paralleling the party organizations in the provinces and main regional areas are the provincial governments which have been officially reorganized and added to since 1928. There are now twenty-eight provinces, exclusive of the dependencies of Tibet and Mongolia. These include six newly created by the national government of Nanking, namely, Hsik'ang (formerly the western marches of Szechwan and part of eastern Tibet), Ch'inghai or Kokonor, Ninghsia (part of Kansu and western Inner Mongolia), Suiyuan, Chahar, and Jehol, which last constitutes the fourth Manchurian province. Chihli ("direct control"), the former metropolitan province has been renamed Hopei ("north of the river"), while Fengtien ("in obedience to heaven") has been changed to Liaoning, referring to the Liao River.

The province was considered by Dr. Sun as a link between the central government and the district unit of self-government, the *hsien*. By the revised law of February 3, 1930, the governmental control of a province is to be in the hands of a group of councilors—seven to nine in number—appointed by Nanking and presided over by a chairman named by the central government. Neither chairman nor councilors may, theoretically, hold administrative office concurrently in another province. The councilors are, of course, to rule in accord with the principles of the Kuomingtang and the mandates of the national government. Bearing in mind what has been said regarding the branch political councils, the *tangpu*, and the powers of the generals, it is clear that, for the time being, the laws regarding the provinces, and their subdivisions, merely set a goal toward which the government may advance with the passage of time.

The policies and aims of the Kuomingtang and of the national government are to be found outlined in the writings of Dr. Sun, in the Canton manifesto of 1924, in the party program laid down by the Extraordinary

Congress of the party held at Canton in October, 1926, and in speeches and mandates of the party and government leaders since the autumn of 1928. These fall into two main divisions, domestic and foreign. Domestic policy aims at the supremacy of civil over military government; the establishment of a uniform policy and economy for the entire country based on honest and effective administration; the abolition of arbitrarily imposed taxes and duties, and the bringing-in of a uniform system of taxation based in part on a progressive income tax and the reform of land taxes; the improvement of land and water communication and transportation, and the development of new harbors; a reform of the educational system, including the incorporation in the state system of all private and Christian mission schools, the regular payment of teachers, and popular education for the masses; the uniform control of all armed forces, and the suppression of banditry and communism; equal political, social, and economic rights for women; the development of industries; aid to farmers by reductions in rent, systems of irrigation and afforestation, and the founding of farmers' co-operative societies and agricultural banks.

Foreign policy calls for the raising of the country from what is declared to be a semicolonial status to that of a fully sovereign member of the family of nations. This includes the revision, or abrogation, of the "unequal treaties" signed by China between 1842 and 1918, the complete control by the government of the customs administration with tariff autonomy, the restoration to Chinese control of the foreign-administered concessions and settlements, and the abolition of extraterritoriality.

Considerable progress has been made by the minister of foreign affairs, Mr. C. T. Wang, in the revision of old, and the negotiation of new, treaties, and the settlement of foreign problems.[1] Less has been accomplished toward a solution of the innumerable problems of a domestic nature, but a start has been made along many lines.[2] Struggles within the government and a recrudescence of civil wars have seriously interfered, so that the solution of many of the problems remains on paper as a guide to the future, instead of having been put into practice. Nor has sufficient time elapsed to allow of evaluation of what has been accomplished. Under the most favorable of circumstances several decades must pass before more than a small part of the program for so vast an area can be realized.

[1] Cf. H. B. Morse and H. F. MacNair, *Far Eastern International Relations*, chap. xxx. Boston: Houghton Mifflin, 1931.

[2] Cf. Tyau, *op. cit.*

CHAPTER XI

NATIONALIST CHINA, 1928-31

CONCERNING no country is it more necessary to keep in mind the difference between theory and practice than in that of China. This truism appears not always to be understood even by the Chinese themselves, who often look upon an order, a plan, or a legal or constitutional provision as synonymous with the application of the principle contained therein. It is, unfortunately, too often overlooked by those outside the country.

Officially China was united under the Nationalists by the conclusion of the northern campaign in the summer of 1928. In reality it was not. Officially the government instituted on October 10, 1928, ruled the country; actually it was no more than the only government at the time which claimed to be the legitimate ruler of all China. The territories fairly definitely controlled by Nanking included most of the five provinces earlier ruled by Sun Ch'uan-fang, namely, Kiangsu, Chekiang, Fukien, Anhwei, and Kiangsi.

The extremely uncertain relations existing in 1928, following the capture of Peking, between Nanking and the provinces along both political and military lines have been indicated. Similar uncertainty prevailed—and, to a considerable degree, still prevails—financially, if Minister T. V. Soong's reports to the Fifth Plenary Session of August, 1928, to the Military Conference held at the capital in the following January, and to the

Third Plenary Session of the Central Executive Committee held in Nanking in March, 1930, are to be accepted. To the Military Conference he stated that of all the country's provinces and special districts only Kiangsu, Chekiang, Anhwei, and Kiangsi furnished financial reports which were "fairly complete or reliable," and added that "many of the provinces do not furnish any reports at all, and those that do, supply data which are either incomplete or of little use." He further remarked that inasmuch as the receipts of Kiangsi and Anhwei were scarcely sufficient to meet their military expenditures, the central government was forced to depend practically upon Kiangsu—in which the capital is located—and Chekiang. He pointed out, incidentally, that of the estimated gross national revenue of $457,-000,000 (silver), 78 per cent of the net revenue was absorbed by military expenditures. He added:

What has so far been proposed in this Memorandum presupposes that financial unification will be achieved. If we are to face existing conditions, we find that facts are quite otherwise and there is chaos in national finances. There is today [January, 1929], little if any improvement from conditions existing during the period of warfare. Thus the national revenues from such provinces as Hunan, Hupeh, Kwangtung, Kwangsi, Shensi, Kansu, Honan, Shansi and Suiyuan, not to mention those from the Three Eastern Provinces [Manchuria], Szechwan, Yunnan, and Kweichow, are entirely appropriated by the localities mentioned. In the Provinces of Hopei (Chihli), Shantung, and Fukien, the revenue officials are at least commissioned by the Central Government, but in other provinces they are appointed by local and military authorities and most of them fail even to render accounts.[1]

On March 1, 1930, Mr. Soong submitted his report on national receipts and expenditures for the year July,

[1] Cf. memorandum quoted from the *North China Daily News*, January 16, 1929, in *The China Year Book* (1929-30), pp. 637-41.

1928—June, 1929. By the summer of 1929, as a result of the withdrawal of the Japanese forces from Shantung, the forced retirement of Feng Yu-hsiang, and civil war in Central and Southeastern China, the provinces of Shantung, Honan, Hupeh, Hunan, Kwangtung, Kwang-si, Kiangsi, and Fukien had been brought under the more or less effective control of Nanking. But Szech-wan, Yunnan, Kweichow, Shansi, Jehol, Suiyuan, Chahar, Shensi, Kansu, Sinkiang, and Manchuria were still not under the control of the central government with the exception of the customs administration.[1]

It is expedient now to analyze the problems and conditions faced by the Nationalist government from the autumn of 1928 to the spring of 1931, to which reference in the broad has previously been made. The members of the Military Disbandment Conference, to which Minister Soong reported so frankly on the financial condition of the government, assembled in Nanking at the close of the year 1928. Much was hoped, but perhaps not expected, from the first gathering of the country's leading militarists since the fall of the Man-chus in 1912. A majority of the leading men of both party and government were present as well as the out-standing generals—Chiang, Feng, Yen, Li Chi-shen, Li Tsung-jen, and Ho Ying-ch'in. The young Marshal Chang Hsueh-liang of Manchuria was not present but was represented inasmuch as he was a member of the State Council and had recently raised the Kuomingtang flag in his satrapy.

A not too subtle appeal to the patriotism of the gen-erals was made by President Chiang in an address to the

[1] Cf. Minister Soong's report as incorporated in Tyau, *op. cit.*, pp. 147-75.

nation on New Year's Day, 1929. In it he compared the weakness of China with the strength of Japan; the latter he attributed to the unselfishness of the Japanese military of the nineteenth century which he contrasted with the selfishness of the Chinese warriors of the twentieth century. He called on the latter to dissolve their armies and unite in working for the good of the country. This appeal to patriotism was followed by Minister Soong's economic appeal based on the impossibility of the country's continued expenditure of so great a part of its finances on armies and wars. As a result of the government leaders' appeals and diplomacy, what appeared for the moment an excellent start was made by the Conference on January 17; on this date resolutions were publicly announced calling for the division of the country into six regions in which disbandment was to take place, namely, Mukden (Chang Hsueh-liang), Taiyuan (Yen), Loyang (Feng), Wuhan (Li Tsung-jen), Nanking (Chiang), and the three practically autonomous provinces of Szechwan, Yunnan, and Kweichow in the west and southwest. The armed forces were to be reduced to 65 divisions of 11,000 men each—which would still cost the country $192,000,000 annually to maintain. In the face of military outbreaks which began a month later the plan proved theoretical and abortive.

From late September, 1928, when the remnants of Chang Tsung-ch'ang's forces were dispersed in Shantung and Chihli, following the capture of Peking in June, to late February, 1929, when Chang Tsung-ch'ang returned from Dairen to Lungkow and Chefoo to attempt to re-establish his power in Shantung, there was peace in China—except for the Mohammedan rebellion in the northwest; continued war against the Communists in eastern Kwangtung, in Hunan, and in Kiangsi; a revolt against Feng Yu-hsiang by one of his generals who moved into Anhwei to create general havoc; a war between Tibetan tribes on the west frontier of Szechwan; a revolt among the Mongols of Barga, on the northwestern border of Manchuria; and innumerable bandit and piratical raids in various provinces, including Kiangsu itself. These last included the kidnapping or murder, or both, of numerous foreigners and natives. The latter, being more numerous and having no shadow of protection by a powerful government, suffered much more than the foreigners.

The application of the new rules for disbandment appeared imminent when Marshal Feng, Nanking's minister of war, suddenly withdrew from the Nationalist capital, on February 7, 1929, for the avowed purpose of putting them into effect in his own satrapy. It shortly appeared, however, that he had left in order to be ready to seize control of that part of Shantung, especially Tsingtao, held by the Japanese as soon as the latter should withdraw. To prevent this the Nanking government was forced, on or about April 4, to request the Japanese to postpone for a time their retirement until its own forces could take over the area relinquished by the Japanese. The latter, accordingly, graciously remained until May 14.

This humiliating state of affairs was brought about by the outbreak of two wars, in February and March, and the threat of a third. The first was caused by the return from Dairen of Chang Tsung-ch'ang, the northern bandit war lord above mentioned; after a two months' struggle he failed to win Shantung and withdrew again to safety in Dairen under the protection of the Japanese. The second war was with that section of the Kwangsi faction ensconced at Wuhan under Li Tsung-jen. Trouble between Nanking and the Kwangsi generals, Li Tsung-jen, Li Chi-shen, and Pai Ch'ung-hsi, had been breeding since the dispute at the Plenary Session over the branch councils in August of the preceding year. The cause of difficulty appears to have been partly personal and partly doctrinal; it was a recrudescence of the age-old struggle in China between centralized and decentralized government, and was intimately connected with the question of national versus provincial (or regional) disposition of revenues. The renewal of the quarrel occurred on February 13—six days after Marshal Feng's precipitate exit from the capital—when the Central Political Council at Nanking refused approval of the Wuhan Branch Political Council's proposal that it supervise (use) the national revenues in the area under its control. To intimate its disapproval of the stand taken by Nanking, the Branch Council at Wuhan dismissed, on the twenty-sixth, the Nanking-appointed chairman of the Hunan government who was a supporter of Chiang and who was shortly attacked at Changsha by a Kwangsi army.

Contemporaneously with the renewal of civil war in Shantung and Hunan, Nanking was preparing for the third regular session of the Kuomingtang Congress. The question of membership in this session of the party Congress was of extraordinary importance on account of the renewal of the quarrel between the right and left wings of the party. The former was in control of the

Central Executive Committee and was determined to remain so. Although it was reported that President Chiang was in personal sympathy with the left, he was officially bound to the right. Early in February (1929) the president delivered an address in which he made clear his hope that Mr. Wang Ching-wei would not return from exile to attend the Congress. Mr. Wang still headed the left wing, whose members were now known as Reorganizationists. To maintain the preponderance of the right wing in the Congress, the Central Executive Committee ruled that it would name substitutes for absent members, and appoint representatives for the overseas party groups. The outcome was that 42.5 per cent of the membership of the Congress were government appointed and, since many of the Reorganizationists absented themselves from a meeting to which they would not have been welcomed, the ruling group controlled a large majority when the Congress was convened on March 15. The natural result was a charge by the left Reorganizationists that the Congress was packed, a charge to which color was given by the amendment of article 29 of the party constitution of January 28, 1924 (as amended on January 16, 1926), to read: "Regulations concerning the organization of the Convention, the election of delegates, and the apportionment of representation in the Convention, shall be made by the Central Executive Committee." This shifted the center of power permanently from the Congress, where it had hitherto reposed in theory, to the Central Executive Committee—in reality, of course, to the Standing Committee of the Central Executive Committee, where it had actually been for the past five years.

The Congress was in session March 15–28 (1929). The quarrel with the left Reorganizationists and the break with the Kwangsi faction prevented the accomplishment of anything of a fundamental nature. No steps were taken toward limiting the arbitrary power of the party and the government, or of granting rights and guaranties to the people and training them for self-rule. In so far as a course of action was laid down, it was a middle one between the laborers and peasants, on the one hand, and the Chinese capitalists, on the other. Little or no encouragement was given to either.

The Central Executive and the Supervisory committees and the Political Council were reorganized. In an attempt to placate other factions and safeguard the "legitimacy" of the one in control, Mme Sun Yat-sen, who was in opposition to the entire party, and Wang Ching-wei, the leader of the left, and Feng Yu-hsiang and Yen Hsi-shan were included in the Central Executive Committee, the three men being appointed to membership in the Central Political Council. The leaders of the Kwangsi faction, having been expelled from the Kuomingtang, were omitted. One of them, Li Chi-shen, the ruler of Canton, was arrested at Nanking and interned, on March 21, when he arrived to participate in the Congress and to mediate on behalf of the Wuhan generals—an instance of illegal and arbitrary action on the part of Chiang Kai-shek which caused much criticism.

As the Russian General Blücher had largely planned the campaign to the Yangtze in 1926, so the German Colonel Max Bauer, President Chiang's personal military adviser, planned the campaign against the Wuhan-

Kwangsi faction in 1929. Two days before the Party Congress adjourned President Chiang left Nanking to direct the Wuhan campaign. The Kwangsi leaders had expected Marshal Feng, who had resigned the war portfolio on March 12 and failed to attend the Congress, to intervene on their behalf. Nanking, however, called on Feng for aid and, possibly, promised him Hupeh if he replied favorably. He sent his troops into Hupeh from Honan, but, before he could reach Hankow, President Chiang arrived there on April 9 as the victor over the Kwangsi rebels. Feng was now as disappointed as the Kwangsi generals had been when he failed to come to their aid.

Li Tsung-jen and Pai Ch'ung-hsi fled to their native province to start an offensive against Canton which they almost succeeded in taking before they were repulsed on May 22. Incidental to this southern campaign was the invasion of the province of Kweichow in May by the Yunnanese troops who were ostensibly aiding Nanking against Kwangsi. The independent governor of Kweichow lost his life, and the province suffered greatly at the hands of the Yunnanese until it came under the control of autonomous Szechwan early in July when the invaders were expelled to their native province.

Having failed to get control of either Hankow or Tsingtao, Marshal Feng, although still a member of the Central Executive Committee, was in a sultry mood. Early in May he began consolidating his position against Nanking by destroying bridges and tunnels on the Lunghai and P'eiping-Hankow railways. On the twenty-fourth a government mandate was issued announcing a punitive expedition against him. On the following day

President Chiang sent a telegram to Feng's generals in which he drew their attention to the fact that their commander had, during the course of years, revolted against his superiors one after another. Two other points covered by Chiang throw considerable light on the situation faced by Nanking at this time: "Perhaps you are not acquainted with the fact that since the conclusion of the Northern Punitive Expedition, the revenues from the provinces of Shantung, Honan, Shensi and Kansu, and the income accruing from the P'eiping-Hankow and the Lung-Hai Railways have been entirely placed at the disposal of Feng. In addition, the Central Authorities regularly remitted $500,000 each month to him. Since the launching of the Punitive Expedition against Wu-Han, the monthly appropriations have been increased to one million and a half. Even for the current month the Central Authorities have paid over five hundred thousand dollars. . . . . Although Feng has been trying every day to refute reports of his relationship with Soviet Russia, in the end his actions will substantiate the reports. We dread the Communists more than we do the sweeping floods and fierce beasts."[1] The message ended with the announcement of the dismissal of Feng from his "substantive and concurrent posts." The latter, and some of his officers, replied with a call upon Chiang to resign, and the announcement of a punitive expedition against him. Considerably less as a result of Chiang's appeal to the Kuominchun generals to desert their commander than from the diversion of funds from Feng to two of his generals, Han Fu-chu and Shih Yu-san, the latter, with a few of their troops, deserted

[1] *The China Year Book* (1929–30), p. 1211.

Feng, and announced their adherence to Chiang. The latter now telegraphed Feng, suggesting that he should either openly revolt or go abroad for a period to widen his knowledge or improve his health—after which he might be restored to grace.

The detachment of two of Feng's generals might have strengthened Chiang and his government had it not immediately been made evident that Yen Hsi-shan was sympathetic to Feng. In a message to the latter Yen declared that he loved the country, the Kuomingtang, and Feng "equally," and invited Feng to join with him in surrendering his forces "to be reorganized according to the decisions of the Reorganization and Disbandment Conferences," and in going abroad. "The mountains are movable but this desire of mine cannot be changed," Yen declared. "If you agree with me, I shall immediately telegraph the Central Government so that orders of advance may be stayed. One of our ancient sages said: 'Lay down your sword and you are comparable to the Buddha.' You possess wisdom and will, I am sure, consider my words. I am awaiting your instructions."

Not since December, 1924, when Marshals Feng and Chang Tso-lin had engaged in a competition in self-effacement, had there been such a display of apparent self-abnegation—and this display of modesty was no more sincere than the earlier one. There was little evidence to warrant a belief that the sometime Christian general had a desire to rival the Buddha. What was made clear was that the two actual rulers of Northern China proper were allies, and that Chiang was checkmated. Nanking was unprepared to conquer the war lords together, and could not have managed their territories at the moment if they had laid down their powers.

There occurred now a pause in the country's chief occupation to permit the removal of Dr. Sun's body from the Pi Yün-ssu, outside Peking, to its final resting place in the magnificent mausoleum built by the government on Purple Mountain without the walls of Nanking. The diplomatic representatives of the foreign powers attended the state funeral on June 1 (1929), thereby contributing added prestige to the national government. Mme Sun returned from her self-imposed exile to attend the ceremonies, and was received with due respect. Until her return to Europe in September she publicly maintained the attitude of criticism of the party, the government, and Chiang Kai-shek which she had assumed two years earlier on the fall of the Wuhan government. She declined to reside in the capital to allow her prestige to be exploited by the government, and criticized the latter for publishing her name among the members of the Central Executive Committee as a means of deceiving the public; she accused the government of being nothing more than one composed of militarists and counter-revolutionists who slaughtered the youth of the land, oppressed the "starving masses," and benefited officeholders who a few years earlier had been poor men but who were now riding about in fine motor cars and purchasing great houses in the foreign settlements and concessions to hold their concubines. President Chiang, her brother-in-law, she bitterly accused of betraying her husband's last instructions while paying them lip-service.

The entombment of Dr. Sun's body was followed in

a few days by the convening of a plenary session of the recently appointed Central Executive Committee of the Kuomingtang. Certain of the measures which the Party Congress had had no time, or will, to consider in March were taken up, particularly those having to do with the education of the people in the principles of the five-power system incorporated in the Organic Law of October 4, 1928, and the preparation of the people for local self-government which should equip them for the third, or constitutional, stage of the revolution. The disillusionment through which the enthusiasts of 1926–27 were now passing, the widespread criticism of the arbitrary actions of the government, the difficulty experienced in discriminating between the advantages of the military government at Nanking and those in other areas of the country to the north, south, and west, and the uncertainty prevailing on account of the military situation in the same areas led the Committee to limit somewhat hesitatingly and apologetically the duration of the period of tutelage. The six years 1929–35 were declared to constitute the length of the period, and the hope—rather than the expectation—was expressed that this would suffice; failing which "it will augur well neither for the Party nor for the whole country."

At the end of June President Chiang went to P'eiping to attempt to detach Yen from Feng. On the twenty-first it had been announced that Feng would be allocated $3,000,000 (silver) for payment of his armies and $200,000 (silver) to cover the expenses of a trip abroad. On the twenty-sixth Feng reached Yen's provincial capital, Taiyuan, and apparently succeeded in strengthening the bond with Yen, inasmuch as the latter refused at the P'eiping conference to break with him. On July 5 the Nanking State Council found it expedient to cancel the order for Feng's arrest; two days later Marshal Chang Hsueh-liang arrived from Mukden to confer with Yen and Chiang. On account of external as well as internal factors nothing constructive was accomplished.

The Kuomingtang has never become deeply rooted in the provinces north of the Yangtze as it has in varying degrees south of the great river. The hold of Chang Tso-lin on Peking and the government established there by him had been essentially artificial and temporary in its nature. It had collapsed owing to Chang's weakness and the short-lived formal affiliation of Yen and Feng with the Kuomingtang rather than because of the part played by Chiang and the southern Nationalist armies. Nor has P'eiping ever been reconciled to the loss of prestige and wealth which it enjoyed as the national capital; demoted to the position of a provincial capital, it remains irreconcilable. Whatever Kuomingtang influence there was in this area in 1929 was mainly Reorganizationist.

While Chang Hsueh-liang had announced allegiance to Nanking, and was willing to allow the central government a voice in determining his foreign policy, he had no vision of abdicating his position by accepting dictation in the internal affairs of Manchuria. This, or the turning-over to him of the control of the northern satrapies of Yen and Feng, would have been the next logical step had the two latter war lords been eliminated at this time. Neither alternative was pleasing to Nanking and Chiang in 1929. Nor was Chang Hsueh-liang at the moment prepared to intervene actively in affairs south of the Great Wall as his father had done with disastrous consequences. It became clear, therefore, that in a war between Chiang and Feng (and Yen) Chang Hsueh-liang would play a neutral rôle such as Feng had played during the recent Kwangsi fiasco.

Moreover, a struggle with the soviets for control of the Chinese Eastern Railway had already been begun on May 27 by police raids on the Russian consulates at Manchouli, Tsitsihar, Harbin, and Suifenho; on July 10, while the three generals were closing their conference in P'eiping, the Chinese Eastern Railroad telegraph and telephone lines were seized by the Chinese, and various soviet organizations were closed throughout the railway zone. On the eleventh the conferees left P'eiping, and nine days later Nanking broke diplomatic relations with the soviets. General Blücher, who had been so helpful to the Nationalists in 1926, was shortly appointed commander of the far eastern forces of the soviets, and in mid-August he instituted military operations against his former colleagues in China.[1]

For slightly more than two months internal war was averted, owing in part to the serious state of affairs in northern Manchuria, and to a degree of uncertainty as to which of the opponents might win in a resort to arms. During the third week in September, however, Chang Fa-k'uei, who had been relatively quiet since his exploits in Kwangtung at the end of 1927, created a diversion which was helpful to Feng and the Kuominchun. Chang and his "Ironsides" were stationed at Ichang; on being ordered by Nanking to transfer to the Lunghai

[1] For the course of this external struggle cf. Morse and MacNair, *op. cit.*, chap. xxx; also *Survey of International Affairs*, 1929, pp. 344-69.

railway zone, he started instead to advance south through Hunan to Kwangsi with the object of continuing on to capture Canton. Cashiered by Nanking on the twenty-first, he immediately received the blessing of Wang Ching-wei and the left Reorganizationists. Nanking answered this defiance on October 3 with an order for the arrest of the leaders of this group. Chang's successes in the south, which were accompanied in the north by a declaration early in October of hostilities in Honan by Feng's leading general, Sun Liang-chen, and a revolt on the seventeenth of the month by the military governor of Anhwei, led Wang Ching-wei, who had recently returned from Europe, to declare, on November 28, his intention to establish a Reorganizationist-Kuomingtang government in Canton. This was delayed by Chang Fa-k'uei's defeat early in December which prevented his capture of Canton.

Late in October President Chiang had personally assumed the leadership of the government forces against the Kuominchun. Partly by military victories, which brought Loyang under national control and forced the Kuominchun to retreat to Shensi; partly, apparently, by a further customary grant of funds to the enemy; and partly, it may be, on account of the hostilities with the Russians in Manchuria the war with the Kuominchun was temporarily suspended at the end of November. Before this, however, General Shih Yu-san, whose loyalty to Nanking had been purchased by Chiang slightly over five months earlier, had received a new inspiration which led him to revolt on October 3, at Pukow, across the river from Nanking, and attempt the capture of the national capital. Narrowly failing in this, he seized all available rolling stock, and retreated northward one hundred miles to Pengpu in Anhwei. The national government barely escaped destruction in this coup.

President Chiang, having closed the campaign against the Kuominchun, hastened back to Nanking, which was badly shaken. His equilibrium was further threatened on December 4 by another mutiny—this time in Anking, the capital of Anhwei, the troops in which joined those of Shih Yu-san at Pengpu. Simultaneously mutinies took place at Changchow, seventy-five miles southeast of Nanking on the railway, and at a point on the north bank of the Yangtze, across from Wusung. From the latter point troops marched to the western edge of the Shanghai International Settlement where they were disarmed on the fifteenth. Ten days before this T'ang Sheng-chih, who had aided the Nationalists in 1926, been ousted in 1927, and restored to the fold in 1928, issued a manifesto, conjointly with several northern generals, denouncing the Nanking government. With admirable impartiality Wang Ching-wei pontificated for this movement as he had for that of Chang Fa-k'uei a few weeks earlier in the south. So imminent appeared the collapse of Nanking that several vessels of the British navy appeared off the water front of the capital to remove foreigners who had returned to their work here following the settlement of the incident of March, 1927.

The national government survived, owing in part to the neutrality of Yen Hsi-shan, but mainly, it appeared, because of Wang Ching-wei's support of the unnatural alliance of T'ang and the northerners; the latter disliked the dictatorship of Chiang Kai-shek and his cen-

tralization schemes for the national government but
they hesitated as yet to contaminate themselves with
the radicalism of Wang and his southern Reorganizationists. On December 12 that part of the Kuomingtang
in control at Nanking solemnly expelled Wang Ching-
wei from the party, and six days later President Chiang
announced the confusion of all his, and his government's, enemies. On the twenty-first Marshals Yen and
Chang Hsueh-liang formally declared their loyalty to
Nanking and their willingness to participate in the
restoration of order. Marshal Feng for the time contented himself with following the precedent of B'rer
Rabbit in a pinch, that of lying low and saying nothing.

That neither Yen nor Feng were spent forces and that
Nanking was to have merely a breathing period between
bouts with both north and south became evident within
two months. Late in February, 1930, rumors became
current of renewed activity on the part of the Yen-Feng
armies. Early in the following month the Kuominchun
armies began moving again into Honan to seize Kaifeng.
On April 3 Yen broke with Nanking by assuming the
post of commander-in-chief of the northern antigovern-
ment coalition, having previously taken over control of
the wireless station in P'eiping and the northern end of
the P'eiping-Hankow Railway, and announced his determination to take over the customs administration at
Tientsin. Feng was to be Yen's deputy while Wang
Ching-wei was now recognized by Yen as the legal head
of the Kuomingtang. A promise was made that the
northern government-designate would call a people's
convention such as Dr. Sun had advocated. Nanking
immediately denounced Yen for his perfidy and ordered

his arrest, but did not attempt to enforce its order. The establishment of a rival government at P'eiping was made manifest by the opening, on May 1, of the offices of the old ministry of foreign affairs in the former capital. Wang Ching-wei did not leave Hongkong to cooperate with the new P'eiping government until midsummer, being as hesitant, it appeared, to ally himself with the northerners as the northerners had been a few months earlier to ally themselves with him.

After weeks of hesitation and preparation Nanking opened its campaign early in May with an attack on Chengchow, in eastern Honan. For more than five months the struggle went on with the most severe fighting that modern China has witnessed. At the outset the northern coalition appeared to enjoy the advantage, profiting by the irresponsible and arbitrary actions of the *tangpu* which had rendered the Nanking Kuoming tang abhorrent to most of the northerners. President Chiang himself was personally disliked on account of his powerful position and his policies, and was hampered by the renewal of military hostilities in the south where the Kwangsi faction and Chang Fa-k'uei's "Ironsides" were campaigning and the Communists were expanding their power in Kiangsi and southern Hupeh. Late in June Tsinan fell to the northerners. But superiority in prestige, funds, arms, and munitions lay with Nanking, and in mid-August its armies retook the Shantung capital. At the end of August Marshal Chang Hsueh-liang, who had refused to join a government set up by his father's old enemies, let it be known that he would intervene; this he did three weeks later, taking over Tientsin and P'eiping. Before announcing his decision, however, the

young marshal had been promised control of the ports
north of the Shantung peninsula, which meant that he
was now ready to attempt the rule of the northeastern
provinces of China proper along with his four Manchurian provinces. By the middle of September the
rout of the northerners was in full swing, and, on
October 13, President Chiang announced the conclusion
of another victorious campaign.

The severity of the fighting during the summer of
1930 against Yen and Feng was manifested by the esti-
mate of the Nanking generalissimo that he had suffered
90,000 casualties and his opponents 150,000.

Marshal Yen now had the opportunity to put into
effect his plans of the preceding year for travel abroad—
having mulcted his province of Shansi, it was charged,
of $80,000,000 (silver) during his twenty years of ad-
ministration. The charge may or may not be true, but
if it were true it may be said in his defense that he had
given peace and good government to his province such
as no other had enjoyed during the "republican" period.
He withdrew at the end of the year to Dairen, and later
crossed to Japan.

Marshal Feng, still unwilling to seek comparison to
the Buddha, announced no plans for withdrawal from
the troubled scenes of his influence but withdrew most
of his loyal forces to his barren, but relatively inac-
cessible, stronghold, Shensi. Mr. Wang Ching-wei, followed a rift between his own left-wing followers and the
Reorganizationists under Ch'en Kung-po, started forth
upon still another pilgrimage to Europe.

The dissolution of the rival government at P'eiping,
and the flight of Wang Ching-wei, had a depressing

effect on the Kwangsi-"Ironsides" rebellion in the south. In keeping with his policy of proclaiming a political amnesty and of bringing peace to the distracted country, President Chiang, in October, deputized General Ma Shao-chun, a native of Kwangsi who was a councilor to the national army headquarters, to go south to attempt a settlement by diplomacy. Not without difficulty, owing to the ambitions and jealousies of the Kwangsi militarists who persisted in guerrilla warfare, were the latter and President Chiang's representative able to come to an understanding. Late in January, 1921, however, General Ma returned to Nanking in company with General Huang Shao-hung, the governor of Kwangsi, and General Chen Chi-tang, commander of the Kwangtung military forces, and plans were immediately formed for the rehabilitation of Kwangsi and Kwangtung, including the taking-over of the "Ironsides" by a government general, as soon as Generals Li Tsung-jen, Pai Ch'ung-hsi, and Chang Fa-k'uei could be persuaded to travel abroad. But the latter were as satisfied to remain in their native land as was Feng Yu-hsiang. While Li remained neutral, Pai and Chang seized the opportunity presented by Huang's absence in Nanking, to seize his capital, Nanning, and set up a new provincial government. Huang returned to the south a month later, having received Nanking's promise of $5,000,000 (silver) for rehabilitation—of which sum he had brought with him $1,500,000. With such means of persuasion it was mistakenly assumed that Huang would be able to win over the recalcitrants.

In the meantime, as a result of the participation of Marshal Chang Hsueh-liang in the crushing of the Yen-

Feng rebellion, an understanding between him and President Chiang had been made which bade fair to work for the interests of the country, if it were maintained. The most skeptical admitted the likelihood of its lasting a year; others, more hopeful, believed that with Chang Hsueh-liang's appointment as vice-commander-in-chief of the Nationalist army, navy, and air force with the charge of reorganizing China north of the Yellow River, and with a closer alignment of the four Manchurian provinces with Nanking, a permanent peace between the two outstanding military leaders of the country was possible. Together the two can prevent Feng Yu-hsiang from breaking the peace and should be able to control the Kwangsi generals. If the more optimistic interpretation be accepted, it may then be argued that the last civil war between the country's old and new militarists has been fought. This does not, of course, preclude the inevitable struggle between the national government and the Communists, whose power and influence appear to have been steadily increasing since the fall of the Borodin-Wuhan government in 1927.

In mid-November (13–18) Marshal Chang Hsueh-liang, who was shortly appointed to membership in the Central Political Council, and President Chiang Kai-shek participated in the Fourth Plenary Session of the Central Executive Committee of the Kuomingtang which considered certain problems of reconstruction ignored by the Party Congress of March, 1929. Following a vigorous and most un-Chinese denunciation by the president of slothfulness and corruption within the party, and of the tyranny of the local branches of the Kuomingtang, plans were made for the implementing of the Control Yuan in the government which has for its objects the impeachment of corrupt and inefficient officials and the auditing of governmental accounts. The latter function will be carried out, it is planned, through an auditing ministry which will have departments in the provinces as well as in the capital. Among the committees appointed to investigate and classify the topics submitted for consideration of the Central Executive Committee were those for political, military, educational, and economic affairs. It was agreed that the central, provincial, and district governments should submit budgets and render reports of their income and expenditures, and that the finances should be reorganized, and foreign and domestic loans liquidated. Plans were laid down for the suppression of communism, banditry, and opium.

One of the means now adopted for the improvement of conditions in the many thousands of villages, in which practically the whole non-urban element in China lives, is that of the *pao-chia*. This is a system under which the inhabitants of a village are to be held responsible collectively for the misdeeds of any of their number who may personally flee from punishment. Like the examination and the control Yuan, it is a return in essence to the doctrine of responsibility which long applied under the empire. Through the official hierarchy and the entire social system—from the Son of Heaven who, on occasion, assumed responsibility for the effects of the forces of nature, to the head of a family—someone was responsible, and punishable, for every illegal action or unfortunate incident which might occur through the length and breadth of the empire.

The reorganization of the army and the dissolution of the Disbandment and Reorganization Committee, so that the army may be directly controlled by the commander-in-chief; the improvement of land and water communications; the abolition of likin by January 1, 1931; the mass education of the people for participation in local government and their preparation for the third stage of the revolution; the abolition of the existing provinces and the substitution therefor of some seventy new ones, calculated to minimize the dangers of feudal regionalism and militarism from which the country has suffered so greatly since 1912; the setting-aside in Nanking of a legation area so that the foreign diplomats may move from the old capital to the new; reorganization of provincial and district party headquarters and the definite limitation of their powers with a view to subordinating them in reality to Nanking; the bringing of education under further control of the party so that it may serve as the handmaid of the government in inculcating the principles of the Kuomingtang, of physical culture, and of natural science among the youth of the land; and the economic rehabilitation of the country along various lines, including river conservancy, afforestation, the opening and development of new ports, and the solution of the agrarian problem—all these were among the problems discussed at the November Plenary Session of the Central Executive Committee.[1] The land problem was of special significance in the light of communistic developments in the central and southern provinces.

[1] Cf. E. B. S. Lee, "Fourth Plenary Session," *North China Herald*, CLXXVII, No. 3303 (November 25, 1930), 282.

Possibly the most important resolution adopted at the Session was that submitted by President Chiang and Messrs. Hu Han-min, Tai Chi-t'ao, Yu Yu-jen, and Ting Wei-fen which called for the opening of a National People's Convention in Nanking in May, 1931. This decision was due in part, undoubtedly, to the similar action taken by the northern rulers in the preceding summer, and in part to the desire of President Chiang to strengthen the government and, possibly, his own position therein. The details involved were left to be worked out by the Standing Committee of the Central Executive Committee. The acceptance of the proposal was a personal triumph for President Chiang, as was the entire session of the Committee, despite the occasional opposition of Mr. Hu Han-min. It was a definite step toward the legitimization and stabilization of the central government and the party group in power; it presented an opportunity to appeal to the country on the basis of Dr. Sun's plans for such a convention when the country should have been united under the Kuomingtang. Coming as it did after the expulsion of Wang Ching-wei and the collapse of the Yen-Feng coalition, it foreshadowed the indefinite rule of President Chiang and his colleagues at Nanking.

On February 28, 1931, a conference was held in the capital to prepare the agenda for the People's Convention. This was composed of the president, the heads of Yuan, the government ministers, and others. President Chiang proposed that the People's Convention in May should consider the promulgation of the provisional constitution which Dr. Sun had advocated for the period prior to the adoption of the permanent constitu-

tion of the third period. Unfortunately the founder of
the Kuomingtang had implied that the provisional constitution should not go into force until local self-government had been established throughout the country.
This was seized upon by Hu Han-min, the president of
the Legislative Yuan, as a ground for opposition. He
argued that the country was not ready for provisional
constitutional rule. Neither Chiang nor Hu would give
way; the result was the resignation of Hu from the
presidency of the legislative Yuan and his concurrent
governmental and party positions. This was accepted
by Chiang, who also ordered Hu's personal detention in
Nanking lest he withdraw to join an antigovernmental
faction, "thus destroying his prestige and long record
of faithfulness to the revolutionary cause,"—as Chiang
himself formally stated on March 9.

It appears that the break between the two men was
not a sudden one. The death of T'an Yen-k'ai, the
president of the Executive Yuan in 1929, had left Hu in
a position in government and party circles second only
to that held by Chiang, and it has been suggested that
he had aspirations toward supplanting Chiang in the
leadership of both. Shortly before the break Hu had
come out strongly in favor of a suggested loan to the
Nanking government of one million ounces of silver by
the American government which he declared would en-
able the government to stabilize finances and enter upon
the economic reconstruction of the country. In taking
this stand Hu appears not to have consulted with his
colleagues, or to have defied them in so doing. He had
earlier criticized the government for the enormous expenditures involved in the northern campaign of 1930,

and had later, it is said, opposed Chiang's plans for a general political amnesty and forced him to modify them in some degree.

Many feared that the promulgation of a provisional constitution would strengthen the executive branch of the government at the expense of the legislative, and enhance the personal prestige and power of Chiang. It is apparent, therefore, that the break between the two chiefs at Nanking symbolized a recrudescence of two principles which have played a part throughout a considerable period of the revolution, namely, personal jealousy and the struggle between the executive and legislative branches.

On March 2 President Chiang issued a formal statement vindicating his stand and criticizing Hu's position: "We have had to pass through many years of bloodshed, many of our comrades have paid the supreme sacrifice and untold millions of our people have suffered in order that a People's Conference may be called for paving the way for the establishment of lasting peace and prosperity. . . . . What are Mr. Hu's intentions that he arbitrarily rejects the right of the people to hold a national convention to discuss the question of a provisional constitution? Is it not clear that without a people's convention and a provisional constitution, the Legislative Yuan would continue to have sole power and authority to make and unmake laws during the period of political tutelage? If this spirit is tolerated, the spirit of the people's convention would be lost and the sacrifices of the party and nation during the last few years rendered in vain."

Undiscouraged by the retirement of Hu Han-min, the

Standing Committee of the Central Executive Committee immediately appointed a Constitutional Drafting Committee. This was composed of Wu Tze-hui (Ching-heng), a native of Kiangsu, one of the elder statesmen of the Kuomingtang, sometimes described as an "intellectual anarchist," who had opposed communism in the 1925–27 period, and had supported Chiang after his break with Wuhan in 1927; Ting Wei-fen, a native of Shantung, a prominent member of the Central Executive Committee, and a member of the Shantung provincial government since 1928; Wang Ch'ung-hui, the distinguished legal authority, delegate in 1921 to the League of Nations Assembly, and to the Washington Conference, also a deputy-judge of the Permanent Court of International Justice; Ts'ai Yuan-p'ei, a native of Chekiang, sometime chancellor of Peking National University and a member of the State Council since 1928; Shao Yuan-ch'ung, also a native of Chekiang, private secretary to Dr. Sun (1916–18), since 1928 a member of the legislative Yuan, since 1929 a member of the Central Executive Committee; Liu Lu-yun, a native of Kiangsi, member of the legislative Yuan since 1928 and of the Central Executive Committee since 1929; Shao Li-tzu, a native of Chekiang, a member of the Central Supervisory Committee since 1926, and chief secretary to Chiang Kai-shek since 1927; Yeh Ch'u-ts'ang, a native of Kiangsu, since 1929 a member of the Central Executive Committee and Central Political Council; and H. H. Kung, a native of Shansi, minister of industry, labor, and commerce since 1928, sometime a member of the Central Executive Committee and Central Political Council, and a brother-in-law to Dr. Sun and Chiang Kai-shek.

Among other matters discussed by the delegates to the People's Convention were the abolition of dictatorships and the establishment of republican government, the carrying to completion of Dr. Sun's reconstruction plans, and the abolition of the special rights and position of foreigners in China. The effects of the break between President Chiang and Hu Han-min and the outcome of the People's Convention remain to be observed.

CHAPTER XII

THE HAMMER AND SICKLE *vs.* THE TWELVE-POINTED STAR

DESPITE the attention generally paid to the principles and organization of the Kuomingtang and the national government at Nanking, it remains a matter of doubt in the summer of 1931 whether the symbol of these, or that of the Communists, is ultimately to mark the flag of China. In 1912 the dragon flag of the Manchus gave place to the five-barred flag of the republic; in 1927 the latter was supplanted by the twelve-pointed star of the Kuomingtang and the Nationalists. That the rulers at Nanking fear the hammer and sickle of the Communists was made abundantly clear by President Chiang Kai-shek when, in his opening address before the Fourth Plenary Session of the Central Executive Committee in November, 1930, he listed the Communists first among the enemies of the government.

Asked in the summer of 1927, when the Wuhan-soviet government was in process of dissolution, what the next development would be, Borodin replied: "The revolution must go underground." He was correct in part: the Communists went underground to the extent that a complete break between them and the Nationalists followed; but from that day to the present there has been no hesitation on the part of the Communists, and no intermission in the development of their campaign.

Directly and indirectly, above as well as under ground, they have harried the people and the somewhat shadowy national government through considerable parts of Central and Southern China. Honan, Hupeh, Hunan, Kiangsi, Anhwei, Fukien, and Kwangtung have been the objects of their special attention, but no part of the country can be claimed to have been unaffected by the Communists, Russian and Chinese. Some two hundred thousand square miles in the heart of the country, inhabited by at least fifty millions of people, have been directly affected.

Since first the soviets turned their attention to the Far East in 1919, discussion has been rife among foreigners in China and the Chinese themselves concerning the fitness of China as a field for Communist effort.[1] The consensus of opinion for a decade was that for four reasons, chiefly, communism could not succeed among the Chinese. Historically, the rule for eighteen years (1068–85) in the eleventh century of the socialist prime minister, Wang Ngan-shih, his fall from power, and the undoing of his work were cited as precedent against a twentieth-century appeal to communism. Second, the fact that China has barely witnessed the birth of industrialism, and has but a small urban industrial proletariat, has made it appear that Marx's prerequisite—a fully developed industrial society—for communism is lacking. China is overwhelmingly, probably 80 per cent, an agricultural country in which class consciousness has been conspicuously lacking. The peasants, it has been

[1] Cf., e.g., H. F. MacNair, "Combating Bolshevism in China," *China's International Relations and Other Essays* (Shanghai: The Commercial Press, 1926), pp. 158–69.

declared by non-peasants, have few needs, no national or patriotic outlook, and are essentially conservative and content. Moreover, the conditions of landowner-ship in Russia prior to 1917 were different from those commonly prevailing in China. In the latter it was esti-mated a few years ago that 90 per cent of the peasants own the lands they cultivate and, it was opined, they would never support the nationalization of their hold-ings in order to carry out the theories of alien Com-munists. Finally, it has often been claimed that the unit of the Chinese social system, the patriarchal family, is *sui generis* unalterably opposed to the radical theories and practices of European Communists.

These arguments are interesting but, in the light of developments in China during the past two decades, they deserve to be considered as hypotheses rather than as axioms. With reference to the example of Wang Ngan-shih, it may be suggested that precedents as such are less compelling in contemporary China than they were in the nineteenth century, and that the groups to whom communism presents an appeal are either not well informed on conditions prevailing eight centuries ago, as in the case of the peasantry, or anxious to make a complete break with their country's past, as in the case of young "intellectual" radicals who have little to lose by the overturn of an ancient system of social organ-ization which has cramped them mentally and eco-nomically.

Concerning the second argument it is to be noted that Russia in 1917 was not much farther along the road of industrialization than is China, but that that lack did not prevent the inauguration of a system of government in Russia which has lasted close to a decade and a half and which shows little sign of passing away. Communism was not established, nor has it been maintained, in Russia on a foundation of the people's will. It was the imposition of a system of thought and government by a zealous and ruthless minority who used methods which the Nationalists copied in China; the membership of the Kuomingtang, it is to be noted again, includes approximately one in one thousand of the population. The will of a few men acting with decision is stronger than the apathy of the masses in any country. It is worthy of remembrance, moreover, that Lenin himself veered away, at least temporarily, from Marxian ideology when he declared in 1920: "One must abandon scientific prejudices that each country must pass through capitalistic exploitation; the power of the Soviets . . . . can be established in those countries in which capitalist development has not attained any serious proportions."[1] Nor should Trotsky's dictum in his *Defense of Terrorism* be forgotten: "Revolution is founded on intimidation—it kills individuals, it intimidates thousands. Thus a conscious minority dynamically converts itself into a majority by slaying its main opponents and terrorizing the rest."[2]

That China is overwhelmingly agricultural—probably 85 per cent—is indisputable, but that 90 per cent of the peasants are landowners is subject to doubt. Statistics in China for practically all native institutions are considerably less conspicuous than are generalizations,

[1] Quoted by M. T. Price, "Communist Policy and the Chinese Nationalist Revolution," *Annals of the American Academy of Political and Social Science*, CLII, 231.

[2] *Ibid.*, p. 230.

guesses, and rumors. Conditions vary greatly from province to province, and even within one province. Nevertheless, a competent foreign observer of conditions in Kiangsi and Hunan a few years ago estimated after careful research that 75 per cent of the peasants were tenants of absentee landlords.[1] In some parts of Northern China more than three-fourths of the farms are said to be owned by the workers, but in considerable areas of the east-central provinces less than 50 per cent are tenant owned. The farms are small—slightly over five acres on the average—and, owing to population pressure, there is less than one acre for the support of each individual. The average income per member of a farmer family, exclusive of house rent, is approximately $2.30 (gold).[2]

To argue that under these basic conditions the people of any country, Oriental or Occidental, can be content appears erroneous. When, however, the passage of armies and bandit gangs back and forth across the country, who seize the crops or prevent sowing and harvesting, who impress into unpaid service all able-bodied men who do not flee their clutches, who rape the women or carry them off, and who plunder and often burn the villages, are taken into account, still more illogical does such reasoning appear. When, in addition, the high degree of provincial autonomy under oft-changing war lords who collect the taxes many years in

[1] Cf. E. Hunter, "The Seriousness and Extent of the Red Armies," *China Weekly Review*, LV, No. 9 (January 31, 1931), 322–25.

[2] J. L. Buck, "Agriculture and the Future of China," *Annals of the American Academy of Political and Social Science*, CLII (November, 1930), 109–15.

advance is taken into account, one can understand why the peasants of China may lend attentive ears to the promises of Communist agents.

Under the conditions prevailing in vast areas of China the common people are easily persuaded that they have nothing to lose by a change in political philosophy and social organization, and are not prone to inquire whether the Communists can make good their promises.

As for the opposition of the patriarchal family to change, it may be remarked that this unit of society was under fire long before the overthrow of either the Manchus or the Romanovs. For more than a century the impact of the West upon the Far East has been acutely felt through both physical and non-physical channels. Modern education, and Christianity itself, sapped the foundation of China's ancient social system before ever Western industrialism rooted itself in the country. If communism had not been introduced, the "big family" must have given way to the "small," owing to the exigencies of the modernizing influences of international intercourse, particularly that of industrialization. Communism is merely an additional factor of disintegration. In old China a largely autochthonous culture flowered and came to fruition. Under no conditions could it have remained static since natural law functions in the East as well as in the West; stagnation has always been a matter of degree rather than of essence. That the patriarchal family is opposed to communism is, therefore, of no permanent significance whatever, there being quite as many non-Communist Chinese liberals who are opposed to it as there are Communist.

Before the consummation of the entente between Dr.

Sun and M. Joffe in 1923, there were Communists in China; following it, the latter grew rapidly in number. Hitherto they had been mainly intellectual theorists playing with an idea; following their admission to Kuomingtang membership they became practical to a degree and as zealous as the proponents of a new religion. Their appeal was directed to the agricultural peasantry in the southern provinces and to the urban proletariat of the ancient handicraft guilds and the modern native and foreign factories of a few partially modernized cities and treaty ports. The working conditions in the latter were no worse—in fact, they were generally better —than in the former. The opportunity for propaganda is better in the modern industrial units, however, owing to the employment in them of larger numbers of laborers who have, in many cases, left their ancestral village homes to live in tenements near their work. The conservative influence of family heads cannot easily make itself felt in the floating population of a modern industrial center. The fact that a considerable number of China's modern mills are foreign owned has rendered it easy for agitators to stir up enmity on an antiforeign basis.

Two important factors in the Communist movement cannot be discussed with any degree of precision—namely, the exact relationship of the Chinese Communists with Russia since 1927, and the percentage of ordinary bandits participating in the rebellions as contrasted with actual converts to communism. Some of those involved appear, indeed, to fall into neither category since it is clear that many have joined both bandits and Communists against their will. Once in, however, it is all but impossible to withdraw, owing to the prevalence of avengers and blackmailers. Escape is possible for a few, but for most the only process of legitimization is the somewhat hazardous one of an army's being bought over *en masse* by the government as an easy, but not always successful, method of squashing rebellion. In the case of the Communists, however, the buying of troops has chiefly been on the side of the rebels since, being cut off generally from the sea, they are dependent for arms and munitions mainly on defeated or disloyal government troops.

There appear to have been few or no Russians among the Chinese Communists since the Wuhan and Canton *débâcles* of 1927. Many of the leaders are young Chinese, some fairly well-educated ones, who have had no training abroad but who have felt the need for revolutionary changes in the social system of their country, and have accepted the philosophy and the promises of Moscow as constituting a basis for change. The ruthlessness of Trotsky's methodology has appealed to them strongly, as has been manifested in the atrocious acts of cruelty perpetrated by them on foreign and native members of the capitalist-bourgeois class. Without attempting to differentiate between brigands and Communists, which under prevailing conditions, is impossible, mention may be made of the looting and burning of Changsha, the capital of Hunan, in the summer of 1930; the holding in captivity for two and a half months of two English women missionaries in Fukien, during the same summer, and their execution under horrible circumstances on September 20; and the execution, after torture, of the Nationalist general, Chang Huei-chan, at Kian, a Communist stronghold in west-central Kiangsi, in January, 1931.

The correspondent of the *North China Herald* in Nanchang, Kiangsi, reported the death of General Chang, under date of February 18, as follows:

> According to the information which the writer has secured from soldiers and officers of the 18th Division . . . . General Chang Huei-chan was first well treated by the Red leaders, for they hoped that he would surrender and fight for them. But their offer was turned down and he began to suffer torture. At first a big hole was cut through his upper lip and he was then made to crawl on the ground confessing his crimes as a General of the Central Government. As he attempted to defend himself and argue with the Red leaders, his tongue was immediately ordered to be cut out. Finally his head was chopped off with an old-fashioned axe and his body was burned with Chinese yellow paper and kerosene oil. [Later] a soldier of the 77th Division . . . . found a big piece of board on which there was a human head wrapped with red cloth with the two ears nailed firmly, floating on the river near Kian. On the board also a few sentences written in Chinese saying, "This is General Chang Huei-chan of the 18th Division and an example for the leaders of the government to whom we shall do the same."[1]

Innumerable other examples of kidnapping or murders, or both, of Chinese and foreigners, and the destruction of their property might be given, only the most picturesque of which are ordinarily reported in the press of Western countries.

Foreign missionaries residing in the interior (it is to be remembered that, with the exception of the diplomats in Peking or Nanking, all other foreign nationals are restricted to residence in the treaty ports with the right to travel only in the interior) and Chinese Christians have been the object of special attention by the Communists, since the former are regarded as the agents

[1] CLXXVIII, No. 3317 (March 3, 1931), 287.

of "imperialism" and the latter are the "running dogs of the imperialists." Communism is avowedly opposed to religion as "an opiate for the people," to quote the phrase of Marx and Lenin. Bandits as such pursue foreign nationals mainly for economic reasons, as a source of replenishment for their exchequers. The Communists, on the other hand, attack Christian missionaries and Chinese converts as representatives of religious and political systems which are their unbending foes. Christianity is the object of special attention not only because it is a religion, but because it is the most virile religion in contemporary China and because of its intimate relation with the "bourgeois" powers of the West. Communism under Lenin's leadership and interpretation developed a Mohammedan-like propensity for appeal to all peoples, regardless of race and color, and particularly to those in a condition of servitude. The treaty basis of Christianity in nineteenth- and twentieth-century China has rendered it peculiarly vulnerable to the criticism of the Communists. Since it is, in addition, supported and led largely by nationals of England, France, and the United States, the Red Terror has made it an object of special opprobrium. If Christian missions can be destroyed, and the missionaries expelled, a great step forward will have been taken by the Russian and Chinese Communists, and to that extent the country will have been prepared to accept the doctrines of Moscow.

If Russians have not personally participated in the Communist campaigns since 1927, they have by no means been indifferent to their course. There had been too much preparation for bringing China into the Russian fold, and the country is too important, as a base for

world-revolution and as a stronghold for capitalist in-
vestment, to be easily relinquished. In 1920 the Second
Congress of the International approved the entrance of
Communists into non-Communist parties when the
former were not strong enough to stand alone. In the
same year a Congress of Oriental Nations, in which
China was represented, was convened in Baku, and the
Third, or Communist, International was encouraged to
persevere in the East by the appointment of a propaganda committee. Two years later the International
convened, at Moscow, the First Congress of the Toilers
of the Far East; this had for its object the completion and
application of the policies of the Congress of Oriental
Nations. A Communist university of the Toilers of the
Orient was now established for formal technical training
of laborer propagandists. In 1925 another institution,
the Sun Yat-sen University, was founded in Moscow for
students of a higher class and grade. In Leningrad,
Irkutsk, and other Russian cities, also, Communist educational institutions were opened to Chinese. To attend
such schools hundreds of Chinese left their country as
others had done, and were still doing, for Japanese,
American, and Western European institutions. In the
meantime the soviet ambassador, Karakhan, had been
propagandizing in the National University of Peking
and other schools and colleges there, and Communist
colleges and "universities" had been springing up in
Shanghai and elsewhere, and Borodin had helped organize at Canton a Political Training Institute.[1] In all these
centers of Communist learning large numbers of Chinese

[1] Cf. e.g., A. N. Holcombe, *The Chinese Revolution*, pp. 163–65, 173–74;
also *The China Year Book* (1928), pp. 1316–17.

received training in theory and propaganda-technique which fitted the more able ones for revolutionary leadership. The almost four years' residence of Borodin in China gave him and his Russian colleagues an opportunity to appeal to the growing numbers of urban proletarians and to the too generally oppressed peasants, to young student enthusiasts who were disillusioned by the repeated failures of attempts to establish sound parliamentary or presidential republican government and the continued dictation of war lords who accomplished nothing constructive, to the soldiers and sailors who are mere pawns in the war game, and to the "intellectuals" who were critical of, and already rebelling against, the age-old social system of the country which seemed to blight and obstruct all modern liberal thought and institutions. The appeal to class consciousness was a clarion call such as had never before been made to all those who travailed and were heavy laden and to those who sympathized with the burden-bearers. It is not to be expected that such influence can pass immediately, especially as the source of communism was far from being exhausted at the time of the breaks of 1927. The continued residence of Chinese students at Moscow, and the return of others to China to apply their theories, has clearly demonstrated this fact. Nor should Mme Sun's pilgrimage to Moscow in 1927, her continued opposition to the Nationalists, and her scorching denunciations of them in 1927 and 1929 be forgotten.

The continued interest of the soviets in the spread of communism in China, and their interpretation of events there, are witnessed *inter alia* by contemporaneous reports in the soviet press. The Moscow *Pravda*, the official

organ of the Communist party, and the most authorita-
tive journal of the soviet capital, in its issue of March
28, 1931, contains an editorial entitled "In the Field of
Class Struggles." It begins by pointing out the enormous "class feats" which have occurred in various countries as a result of the deepening of the crisis in capitalistic countries, and discusses in contrast the enormous
successes of socialistic construction in the Soviet Union.
The bourgeois counter-revolutionists are declared to be
mobilizing for a decisive struggle against (1) their own
proletariat in each country; (2) the nationalistic liberat-
ing movements in colonies—for example, China; (3) the
soviets. Against the bourgeois the masses are rising in
revolution, it is pointed out, and, developing this thought,
the editorial refers to "the strikes, the increasing sweep
of the movement of the unemployed, the rise of the
revolutionary movement in the colonies, and, in particular, the setting up of Soviets and of the Red Army
in broad regions of China." The process of "boring from
within," which the Communists have used for more than
a decade, and which was officially—although, perhaps,
not entirely wittingly—permitted by the Russian-
advised Kuomingtang from January, 1924, to the summer of 1927, has brought results in the "broad regions"
referred to by the *Pravda* editorial.

Three days after the appearance of the *Pravda* editorial, Mr. Al. Hamadan dispatched from Shanghai an
interesting article to the *Young Communist Pravda*
under the caption "The Rickshaw [Man] with a Rifle."
This appeared in the issue for April 16. After referring
to the victory of Nanking over the Yen-Feng coalition
of 1930, he set out to report the results of Nanking's

"boastfully announced Three Months' Plan for the Extirpation of the Communists" in three hundred regions under Red control in Kiangsi, Hunan, Hupeh, and other provinces. Chiang Kai-shek's well-armed Kuominchun and Nanking troops were estimated at five hundred thousand. To face these the Red soldiers were declared to have one rifle for every four or five men, in spite of which, aided by tens of thousands of coolies, rickshaw men, and other workmen, and hundreds of thousands of peasants, they succeeded in repulsing the government armies. "The Chinese proletariat rose to defend with its chest its own army." Sarcastic allusions were made to President Chiang's speeches on the "brilliant feats" of his troops who had not, at the time the speeches were given, met the Red army, but merely peasant detachments acting as scouts, who were reported by the national government as "enormous detachments" numbering eight to ten thousand. "Expensive banquets in Nanking, Shanghai, and Hankow" were described as being given in honor of "the stalwart leader of the liquidation of the Communists," and the "pathos of congratulatory speeches by imperialists, and the lightning flashes of newspaper editorials, and telegrams" which were suddenly replaced by a "period of silence," were ironically commented upon. Then, suddenly, "banquets lost their splendor and the imperialists retreated to cruisers which were waiting. Nothing was heard of events at the front. Censorship, police, and troops cruelly fought against any news of the actual state of affairs which might get through, and it turned out that the Chinese Red army had abandoned the tactic of retreat, of temporary withdrawal to gather force, and had passed to the tactic of lightning-like attacks of a guerrilla type. The generals in their panic began to demand that Chiang Kai-shek appear in person at the front 'to inspire the army.' The army in fact needed inspiration. The soldiers, looked upon as cannon fodder by the generals, hungry and in rags, seeing no end to the fights of the generals, sent to destroy their own brothers—workmen and peasants—took the only proper road, and, in whole detachments, went over to the side of the Red army, taking with them their arms, their gatling guns, and even artillery."

In the same article accounts were given of the part being played by women in the Chinese Communist movement. While many have organized to give medical and other types of aid to the Red army, others such as Ho En and Ho Siang-ku, two sisters of the notorious Ho Lung, are reported to be at the head of fighting forces. The younger of these women, Ho En, is said to have led eight thousand Communists to drive out government troops from two cities in northwestern Hunan and southwestern Hupeh, respectively, and to have aided in the organization of a soviet government in an area with a population of from four to five millions. Elsewhere it is declared that the Reds, having destroyed the "Three Months' Plan," are now preparing for a general offensive.

In the issue of the same journal for April 25 (1931) the Eleventh Plenary Session of the Executive Committee of the Communist International at Moscow was reported. The most important successes of the sections of the International during the past year were summarized under eight headings. Of these the first listed is the creation of soviets and a Red army in China, and the assumption of leadership of the Communist party in the peasant revolution of China and Indo-China. In the Presidium, thirty in number, two Chinese and a Japanese are listed; of the former, Koo An-ping is one of the thirteen members of the political secretariat, which directs the policy of the Communist International.

The stress laid upon the peasant-agrarian aims of the revolution in all reports by the Moscow press of developments in China, Indo-China, and India is extremely significant. By this means the lack of readiness of most of Asia for the Marxian revolution of the proletariat is overcome, and advance toward World Revolution is being made by Moscow.[1]

To the historically minded it is interesting to observe the parallel between the present-day relations of the Nanking national government to the Communists and those of the imperial Manchu government to their Chinese opponents in the middle of the nineteenth century. As a result of the First Anglo-Chinese War (1839–42) the imperial government called on the people to arm themselves against the British "barbarians." When the war was over the Manchus came near being hoist by their own petard, unable as they were to disarm the people and prevent them from turning their arms against the throne. To strengthen itself to gain an immediate victory, the Kuomingtang took in the Communists in 1924, thinking to use and dispense with their services at pleasure. Seven years later the Kuomingtang is fighting for its life against its late ally.

[1] For bringing to my attention the articles quoted in the Moscow press, and for translating them, I am indebted to my colleague, Professor Samuel N. Harper.

Concerning the organization and membership of the Chinese Communist party little is known except that it is organized along the general lines of the Russian party and is functioning on a national scale. Prior to the establishment of the soviet government in Russia the interest of Chinese in communism was almost purely academic; the literature and propaganda began to come in from Japan as well as from Russia.[1] A soviet agent, Popov, reached Shanghai in 1919 to study the situation and report to Moscow. In the following year a Chinese Communist party, the Kungtsantang, was organized, and China was represented at the Baku Congress. In 1921 the Kungtsantang entered into affiliation with the Third International. Membership grew slowly during the next few years although the process of forming cells within the Kuomingtang appears to have been immediately undertaken. Following the official opening of the Kuomingtang to the Communists in 1924, the Kungtsantang expanded fairly rapidly under Russian inspiration and guidance, and ere long the tail was swinging the kite. In 1927, when the Fifth National Convention of the party was held, more than 50,000 members were claimed.

The outstanding native civilian leaders of this period were Li Ta-chao, T'an P'ing-shan, and Ch'en Tu-hs'iu. The scholar Li Ta-chao was probably the Chinese representative at the Baku Congress, although the spelling of the name of China's representative given in the press was "Lai." During the period (1923–26) in which Ambassador Karakhan was propagating communism in the government colleges of Peking, Li was his lieutenant,

---

[1] Cf. H. O. Chapman, *The Chinese Revolution*, 1926–27, p. 45.

being the leader of the Peking Communists. His career
was cut short on April 28, 1927, by strangulation following his capture during the raid on the soviet embassy by
Chang Tso-lin's police.

T'an P'ing-shan, a Cantonese, born in 1887, rose to
influence as the head of the students in Canton and of
the local branch of the Young Socialist League. In
December, 1923, he was a member of the Communist
Congress in Shanghai, representing Canton. During the
following three and a half years he was extremely active
in co-operating with Borodin. Like other avowed Communists, he had alternate innings and outings; he participated in the general strike at Canton in 1925; expelled from the Kuomingtang, he was, in January, 1926,
restored to grace as a member of the Central Executive
Committee by the party Congress. He led in the union-
ization of the peasants and laborers and headed their
bloc. When Chiang Kai-shek carried out his anti-Communist coup in March, 1926, during the temporary
absence of Borodin, T'an, the head of the Communists,
was one of those against whom it was directed. With
the return of Borodin, T'an came back into power, and
was a member of the Wuhan government until its collapse in the summer of 1927. Since that time his activities have been carried on through subterranean channels.

Ch'en Tu-hs'iu, the third of the trio of civilian
Communist leaders of the early period, is a native of
Anhwei, born in 1879. After studying several years in
Japan and France, he participated in the revolution of
1911–12. In 1917 he was a member of the department
of literature of the Peking National University; forced

to leave on account of his radical leanings, he edited
La Jeunesse, and other extremist journals in Shanghai,
for a period. In 1924 he joined the Kuomingtang, but
shortly went over to the Communists. During the
sovietization period of the Kuomingtang he was a member of the Central Executive Committee. Called at
times the "Chinese Lenin," he was considered the head
of the Kungtsantang during the Wuhan period, and co-
operated with Borodin and Wang Ching-wei. Like T'an,
he has been a member of the Third International.

Other prominent Communists (or Communist co-
operators) of this period were Li Lih-san, the Moscow-
trained labor agitator and organizer of the great strike
fund in Shanghai following the Nanking-road shootings
of May 30, 1925; Liao Chung-kai, the labor leader and
finance minister of Canton, and Chen Chiu-lin, a newspaper editor, both of whom were assassinated at Canton
in the summer of 1925; Sze Zung-tung, another editor
and a sometime member of the faculty of a Communist
"university" in Shanghai; Hsu Ch'ien, a lawyer, a writ-
ter, an editor, and a friend who accompanied Dr. Sun on
the latter's last trip to Peking, and later became one of
the violent extremists of Wuhan in 1926–27; Ch'en Kung-
po, who for a time headed the Political Bureau of the
Wuhan government and agitated among the laborers of
Central China so successfully as to embarrass even that
radical government; Teng Yen-ta, a Cantonese graduate
of the Paoting Military Academy, who spent some time
in Germany and Russia, and who also for a period was
the head of the Political Bureau of the soviet-Kuoming-
tang government at Canton and Wuhan; and Ku Meng-
yu, born in Chihli in 1888, a graduate of the University

of Berlin, and, for some years, on the economics faculty of the Peking National University, following which he participated in the Canton-Wuhan government in 1926–27, afterward withdrawing to Europe with Wang Ching-wei. Whether the last four listed are formal members of the Kungtsantang is unclear, but, in the light of their actions, of little consequence.

The Russian-inspired first wave of communism rose during the years 1924–26, to break in 1927; since the latter date the Communists have been moving restlessly in a trough, slowly gathering their forces, it appears, to rise a second time. In some ways their position has been not altogether dissimilar to that of the Kuomingtang in the period 1913–25. Prevented from applying their doctrines through an organized government, they have been forced to retreat for a further period of preparation, both military and propagandistic. If their propaganda and their military activities are jointly considered, it appears that the alternatives faced by Nanking are comparable to those faced by the northern war lords from 1926 to 1930. Two sets of leaders and principles are struggling not merely for supremacy but for existence, since it is evident that no country as homogeneous culturally as China can remain half-Communist, half-capitalist, in organization.

Evidence of this is to be found in such Communist sources as Nos. 1 and 2 of the *China Correspondence*, published by the Revolutionary Red Aid Society in China in November and December, 1930. Composed in somewhat indifferent English and without too great a regard for accuracy of statement, these bulletins contain excellent material illustrative of the appeals of com-

munism to peasants and laborers. In catechetical form
the aims of the Society are presented in No. 1:

1. For what is the Revolutionary Red Aid Society in China
organized?

Whenever the ruled class in any country are brutally oppressed by
the ruling class, the former together with their sympathizers are
bound to [be] enraged. To the brutal oppression, there is always an
equally powerful reaction. . . . . The White Terror is so cruel that
the country-wide masses have to guard themselves against it by
means of organized strenth [sic]. Every day speeches are their
"wills"; bloody clothes are to be the only ornaments left for their
corpses; and this is the sole background of the organization of the
Revolution [sic] Red Aid Society in China.

2. Who are the organizers of the Revolutionary Red Aid Society
in China?

Whoever will profit from the anti-White-Terror movement are
organizers of the movement. It is the whole oppressed class who
want the movement most urgently. So, the organizers . . . . are
workers, peasants, poverized people, students, revolutionary elements and revolutionary sympathizers belonging to the liberal profession. . . . .

3. What is the programme of the Revolutionary Red Aid
Society in China?

It is as follows:

A. Oppose the White Terror, namely oppose all oppressive
measures adopted by the ruling class against all revolutionary movements.

B. Aid all revolutionary struggles . . . . aid all movements
against the ruling class.

C. Aid all revolutionary fighters and their families . . . . summon
the masses to assist the victimized revolutionary fighters and their
families.

D. Summon famine sufferers to demand for relief. Chinese
famine sufferers are products of the Chinese militarist wars. . . . .
What does the migration of famine sufferer mass into city mean? It
means that China is suffering complete bankruptcy of village economy as well as of the economy of the whole country under the rule
of the Koumintang [sic]. . . . .

E. Oppose Fascist philanthropy. . . . . From it the Koumintang
gets most of its military funds. . . . .

F. Oppose imperialists and the Koumintang attacking the Chinese Soviet district. The Chinese Soviet district is the fruit of the present revolution in China. Aiming to completely eliminate revolutionary influence, imperialists and the Koumintang are jointly attacking the area. They have launched many a suppression campaign, they have burned up many forests and bombed many mountains. They kill every body [*sic*] and destroy every thing [*sic*] in their way.

4. How is the Revolutionary Red Aid . . . . getting along at present?

[It] has now a total membership of 730,000, 700,000 in the Soviet district and 30,000 in the White region. The Red Trade Unions, Poor Peasants' Associations, Revolutionary Students' Unions and Poor Women's Associations are all its affiliated members. Only with the exceptions of Tsinhai, Chinese Turkistan, Tibet and Kweichow, its organization has spread over all parts of China. There are, however, several defects about the organization at present: (1) Number of members in the non-Soviet district too is small; (2) Branches of individual members are not organizationally strong; (3) It is still not an organization of broad masses, for in the non-Soviet district there are only 30,000 members. . . . .

5. What is the relationship between the . . . . Society and the Red Aid International?[1]

The Revolutionary Red Aid Society in China is the branch of the Red Aid International in this country. It, directly aided by the latter, submits weekly reports to it for approval and instruction. . . . .[2]

The issue between the "present joint rule of imperialist and Koumintang in China" and the workers and peasants is clearly outlined in the "Opening Speech" of the same bulletin:

In oppressing the working class the imperialist and capitalists have adopted extraordinarily drastic measures such as lockout, part

[1] The Red Aid International is the Chinese section of the International Society for Assistance to Revolutionaries. The largest and most important section of this organization is the one in the Soviet Union which, under the Russian abbreviation M.O.P.R., is one of the most important of the soviet "patriotic" societies.

[2] Pp. 7–9.

time employment, hire of White Russians to replace natives, thus preparing a "hell and grave," so to speak, for the workers. . . . . As a result, Chinese workers and peasants, being deprived of the means of making a humble living, could not but take the control of destiny into their own hands and raise the revolutionary torch as a final means of self-salvation. Now revolutionary outbreaks in China are matters of daily occurrance [sic] which can be seen anywhere and everywhere. Chinese workers and peasants are firmly dedicated to what is called a "victory or death" struggle against the oppressing class. And they will not desist until they are fully set free. . . . . Now, with the Red armies enlarged to 300,000 men and Red districts comprising more than 300 hsiens [i.e., districts—the smallest units of government in the country], the Chinese Soviet Government as composed of workers, peasants and soldiers is fairly able to stand on its own feet and to face the Koumintang government. Moreover, the Chinese Red Army, consisting of workers and peasants, is advancing towards central cities in an endeavor to effect a conjunction with the struggle in those cities. It is fighting desperately with the Koumintang and imperialist armies and navies for the political control of one or several provinces. At the same time, the workers and poverized people in cities are waging large scale struggles as, for example, continuous strikes and demonstrations, in favor of the Soviet Government, thus unquestionably making the rule of Koumintang and imperialist come to a speedy end. . . . .[1]

Contemporaneously with the winding-up of President Chiang's campaign against the Yen Hsi-shan–Feng Yu-hsiang–Wang Ching-wei coalition in North China in October, 1930, the Red Aid Society held an organization conference to prepare for the announced advance by Nanking against the Communists. To this conference one S. A. Dai presented a report[2] analyzing the difference between "two kinds of governments and two kinds of armies." That of the Kuomingtang,˙ he declared, is

hated by the masses. It sells air right, land right, and water right to the imperialists. It has increased the land tax two or three times more than the amount imposed by the Manchus. Besides the land

[1] Pp. 1–3.   [2] Pp. 3–5.

tax, other trivial taxes have numbered over seven hundred. It has within the last three years murdered no less than 150,000 laborers. It arrested and killed more than 5,000 students and teachers last year. It has lately waged a civil war cost among other things, no less than 300,000 human lives and about 300,000,000 dollars Mex. Even the wounded have numbered about 500,000. . . . . Those who still live have to share the burden of about 600,000,000 bonds issued by the Nanking government.

The second kind of political authority is welcomed by the masses. It has lately fought with the soldiers of the imperialists more than ten times. . . . . More than three hundred districts have seen their land confiscated from the hands of the land owners. There are already something like 80,000,000 peasants cultivating land but paying no rent as they used to. In those Soviet districts, about three hundred of them, there is only one single tax, the income tax. Working hours are limited to eight, while wages have been increased lately two to four times. In West Fukien alone, within a territory little over ten districts, there are already three thousand Lenin schools for the peasant children. The Soviets, on the other hand, shoot down anybody who trades in opium.

There are two kinds of wars in China. The first is the fight between the Whites, both sides holding up the Koumintang flags, but each is fighting for its own masters; and the masters for both sides are the imperialists. Such fight among the militarists, though it at present has stopped for a while, will certainly begin again; soon between the Chiang [Kai-shek] and the Chang [Hsueh-liang] factions. The second kind of fight is that of the Reds against the Whites, the Soviets against the Koumingtangs, the "Lower classes" against the "Higher classes"; it is a fight for the masses, decidedly a revolutionary fight.

What did the people receive when the Whites fought the Whites? Land tax was collected in advance, as far ahead as 1943 in some places of Szechwan province.[1] Then there were compulsory labor

[1] This appears to be an extremely conservative statement. Professor Guy W. Sarvis, a member of the Laymen's Foreign Missions Inquiry, who traveled through a considerable part of Szechwan during the first quarter of the year 1931, makes the following statement in his typescript journal, under date of February 8: "In many portions of the province taxes have been collected 30 to 40 years in advance, and in some places it is asserted that they have been collected for 99 years. The people are forced to grow opium and pay a very high tax on it, and if they refuse, they pay the opium tax anyhow— it is then called a 'lazy tax'—a tax which no other crop will support."

and compulsory contribution of various good for the soldiers and for the officers in the White forces. Working hours in the arsenals were prolonged, communication interrupted, rice price rapidly advanced, salt supply almost exhausted! During the fight between the Red and the White, the situation is quite different. The White army burns every thing [*sic*] in sight and kills everybody within reach. The White soldiers are ordered to stuf [*sic*] their ears with cotton, lest they may easily be attracted by the slogans and the songs of the Red army! Whenever the Red force arrives, it eradicates all the evils for the people, and causes new, healthy and useful organizations to be set up. Whenever it leaves, it distributes among the peasants the arms taken from the land owners and Whites. The peasantry is always a formidable force behind the Red army. . . . .

A survey of the military strength and position of the Communists at the close of 1930[1] reported the active operation of eleven armies in, or on the borders of, Honan, Hupeh, Hunan, Kiangsi, Anhwei, Fukien, Kwangtung, and Kwangsi. Another army had been organized, and was preparing for operations in Hupeh; and several others were in process of formation to operate in Hupeh, Hunan, Hopei (Chihli), and Manchuria.

The Communist technique of Moscow of providing political officers to accompany the commanders of the armies is used by the Chinese Communists, as it was by the sovietized Nationalists in 1926–27. Certain of the political officers are former students, as, for example. Tsao Ta-ching, Tseng Ju-hsiang, Hsi Tai-yuan, Teng Hsi-hsien, and Teng Kan-yuan. Others are former Whampoa Military cadets, such as Chou I-ch'un and Tung Wei-min. Two other Whampoa cadets, Hsu Chi-chen and Tsai Shen-hsi, have become commanders of the first and third Communist armies, respectively. Chu Teh, a German-trained militarist of the pre-Nationalist

[1] E. Hunter, *op. cit.*

period, is the commander of the fourth army, the oldest and best known of these forces. Equally well known is his co-operating military officer, Mao Tze-tung. These two men are outstanding leaders of the movement. Almost equally notorious is the peasant commander, Ho Lung, of the second army. Others of the old-style militarists who have gone over to the Communists are P'eng Teh-huai, commander of the fifth army, and Chang Yun-i, a graduate of the Paoting Military Academy, who leads the seventh army. In northern Kiangsi, in the neighborhood of the famous porcelain factories of Kin-Teh-Chen, Fang Che-ming has been active, while Tuan Teh-chang, Liu Yang, and the bandit leader, Kung Ho-chung, have been terrorizing northern and eastern Hunan for many months.

The methods used by the Communists in gaining a foothold in new territory around Hankow are reported by a competent American observer in China in 1930–31 who has had much experience in that country.[1]

Mr. ———. . . . said that two members of the Party would come secretly or quietly to a village, usually with someone who was a Communist who was acquainted locally. They would have meetings at night or in a temple outside the village with a few of the local men who were most favorably disposed, and would get them committed to the program. The main arguments used were three: first, that they ought not to pay rent because they did all the work and the owner did none; second, that they need not pay their debts because the property really belonged to them as much as to the owner; and third, that they got nothing for their taxes, and that, therefore, they should not pay them. Having won the support of a sufficient number, they would placard the town and then go to people one by one and ask them to join the Party. Of course it would be known by this time that it would be unsafe not to join—although once having joined, there is no way to escape, unless the whole group renounces Com-

---

[1] G. Sarvis, *op. cit.*, date, January 14, 1931.

munism, for the methods are those of the Black Hand, and a Party member who is disloyal is killed. The people are thus caught between the Devil and the Deep Sea, and take the alternative which at the moment seems safest. Finally the whole village would be taken over by the Communists, the land seized and reapportioned, often in very small parcels of less than two acres. Then one day there appeared in the village two strangers dressed in foreign overcoats, inquiring for some of the leading men. These were pointed out to them, and the strangers told them that they had been extortionate and oppressive and that they had come to settle the matter with them. Calling the crowd to stand aside, they whipped automatics out of their pockets and shot the men on the spot. Then turning to the crowd, they asked, "Have we done right or wrong? You be the judges. . . . ." At first there was no resistance to the Communists, but later the villagers, and particularly the owners, organized the Red Spear Societies (Hong Tsiang Hwei), and they terrorized the Communists as the Communists had terrorized them. And when the soldiers came, they secured lists of the Communists, and many who had joined through fear were killed or expropriated. The Communists are pretty well cleared out of the region in which Mr. ———— lives, at least so far as overt activity is concerned, but it is unsafe to go out in most of the country around Hankow.[1]

The activities of the Communists along the reaches of the upper Yangtze, in the Hankow-Ichang region, are described at first hand by the same observer:

JAN. 16.—Today we are to steam through the country of the Reds, and are expecting some compliments from them. Along the river bank are bulletin boards with placards in large characters "Down with imperialism"—which means us, or anything in sight,

---

[1] Interesting light on the manner in which manufacturers are caught between the upper and the nether millstones of nationalism and communism is thrown by the same writer in the following incidental comment: "Mr. ———— told me that the Yangtze Engineering Works [near Hankow] are now [mid-January, 1931] closed because Wang Kwang, the owner, says he cannot run under the conditions laid down. This company was one of the best in China, and Mr. Wang is one of the finest Christian business men. Fourteen per cent. of the profits must go to the government and 50% of the balance to the laborers, and the books must be completely open to inspection. The government owes him about three million dollars [silver] on bridge and other contracts."

particularly the present government at Nanking. . . . . In fact, much of the ideology of the Reds is imported; but except for minor changes, the movement seems to me to differ little from the old-fashioned banditry, and to grow out of the same causes. Contented, safe, well-fed people do not become bandits or Reds in this country. I myself have rather objected to the indiscriminate use of the term "Red" to describe all kinds of "opposition." In this case, however, it is inevitable, for they use the red flag and armband and call themselves the Red Army.

Last night we tied up an hour or more before dark. When we asked the captain why, he said that there was bad country ahead which it would take $2\frac{1}{2}$ hours of steaming to get through, and that if we should get stuck or have to anchor in that region, it might be serious. At first I thought he was referring to the character of the river, but he was talking of the Reds—and you will think we talked of nothing else, which might not be so far from the truth! Yesterday we were stuck in the mud for $2\frac{1}{2}$ hours. The officers pointed out the red flags on the bank and said that they were waiting until nightfall to try to board us—all of which gives some point to our guard of marines! No one was allowed to come aboard after dark last night. . . . .

Jan. 17.—The expected incidents did not occur yesterday, but we did anchor early again in order to avoid passing Temple Hill, where boats are regularly fired on, near night-fall. Temple Hill is at the point where the Yangtze takes a sharp turn to the north below Ichang. . . . . This morning we were up and dressed before 7:30 in anticipation of the firing at Temple Hill. The marines were all out with their rifles. Upstairs, the bridge and the officers' quarters is a small fortress completely encased in armor-plate and with a Lewis gun. . . . . We had passed the summit of the hill . . . . when there was a burst of flame on the saddle connecting the hill with its neighbor . . . . the shots fell short. . . . . All our rifles and machine gun got into action, and there was a lively fusillade for some minutes. . . . . It is rather interesting and significant to note how the attitude of foreign powers toward these matters has changed. Not long ago it would have been necessary to get the permission of the admiral to fire under such circumstances. Now we continued for half an hour to fire at every sign of movement in the neighborhood of any of the red flags which are planted at frequent intervals along the bank. . . . . The whole situation has degenerated into guerilla warfare. It is an illustration of what is sure to happen in the absence of recognized government control. . . . .

During my writing this morning, I have jumped up several times to go to the window and read the signs along the river banks. Some are of the vintage of 1927 and some are more recent. Here are a few:

Establish the government of the soldiers, peasants and workers!
Establish the government of the people; overthrow military governments!
Oppose another world-war!
Recover the Concessions and expel foreign soldiers!

The present struggle between the Communists and the national government and the war lords is, as just stated, mainly one of guerrilla warfare. Another observer, previously cited, remarks:

The military tactics adopted by these frenzied fighters are as simple as a schoolboy's primer. When they are strong enough to meet the foe, they meet him. When not, they drop out of the picture, dispersing like raindrops on the yellow surface of the Yangtze, and apparently are as difficult to distinguish from the mass.[1]

In a second desperate appeal for foreign aid against the Communists, Dr. Ida Kahn, one of China's two most distinguished women physicians, writes:

Think not that I am talking in hyperbole! In my province of Kiangsi alone, only three cities have escaped out of eighty-one county seats, and outside of the city limits, these towns have had fighting carried on around them and much damage has been sustained. Many of these towns have been looted and burned several times, and thousands and thousands of people have been killed, while millions upon millions have been made homeless. . . . . In the city of Kian and the surrounding country alone, twenty-six thousand persons were killed. Even from a small town like Kin-Teh-Chen . . . . the loot carried away amounted to over a million dollars, while from Kian, the silver and gold gathered from repeated lootings (from everywhere) is said to have totalled forty millions. . . . . What makes it even worse is that the damage to the property is not only transient but is more or less permanent. In places which are under the control of the Communists, as in Kin-Teh-Chen, all the deeds were burned. The landmarks to all the fields were obliterated and then three mou, or half an acre, of land was allotted to each family. . . . . When the soldiers come to drive them away, there are no

[1] E. Hunter, *op. cit.*, p. 323.

Communists to be seen. Only peaceful farmers are there tilling the soil and quiet artizans carrying on their trade. When the troops are gone, then up spring the bandits and the looting and pillaging go on as merrily as ever. Hence the famous slogan, "Ni lai ngo ch'u Ni ch'u ngo lai! If you come I will go but if you go, then I will come." Can any troops run such illusive creatures to their covers? Never! No never! And the poor soldiers! Who can blame them entirely! Ill fed, ill clothed, and ill paid with wages many months in arrears, what condition of mind and body are they in to meet these spirits so alert and subtle. One minute they drop upon you almost from the clouds and snatch your weapons away, and the next moment they have melted away like the dew and you cannot find any hide or hair of them. Is it any wonder that whole divisions of troops are surrounded and taken by these daring spirits who are usually far inferior in numbers and who are poorly armed?[1]

Each side accuses the other of the most atrocious cruelties to prisoners—and each practices, apparently, what it blames the other for doing. The *China Correspondence* declares:

Far more terrible and cruel than being shot to death is the corporal punishment scarcely heard of in the world which is always applied to the revolutionary victims after their arrests and before their execution. By doing so, the ruling classes aim to get the secret plans of the revolutionary organizations from the victims. The following corporal punishments are widely employed by the different factions of the Kuomintang:

1. Hanging one or two thumbs in the air, loading baskets of bricks or stones across the shoulders or on the feet and then whipping the whole body.

2. Pulling the head, the hands and feet of the victim in different directions in the air by means of a specially made implement and then striking the body with sticks or forcing the victim to breathe in suffocating gas.

3. Beating the back of the victim with hammer or pricking with needles deeply into his hingers [*sic*].

4. Passing strong electric current through the victim's body—this is learned from the imperialists.

---

[1] *China Weekly Review*, LV, No. 13, 446–48; cf. also Chia Hsi Yen, "What Communist Bandits Have Done in Kiangsi," *ibid.*, No. 5, pp. 186–87.

5. "Iron Hat"—a special iron made hat which, when put over the head, can be contracted by screwing and the victim's head is squeezed from all sides.

6. Injecting iron wires into sexual organs, no difference with male or female.

7. Hanging up side down—hanging the major toes in the air and then various cruel actions are played on the body.

8. Stamping the bare body with red hot iron plates until the whole body of the victim looks like roasted meat.[1]

The campaign of the Nationalists against the northern coalition during the summer and autumn of 1930 forced President Chiang Kai-shek to withdraw almost all government troops from the central and southern provinces: this left the Communists practically a free hand to expand their hold by military pressure, propaganda, and the purchase of adherents by money and threats. The ending of the northern campaign offered an opportunity, more apparent than real, to the Nanking government to undertake the crushing of communism. Its troops were worn out by unceasing and desperate war; the government itself was financially embarrassed; how long a time might elapse before it would be called upon to face another war with Feng Yu-hsiang, with the Kwangsi faction, or even a struggle with Chang Hsueh-liang, no one could predict. Plans were immediately announced for the undertaking of the anti-Communist war, however, and parts of the defeated troops of Yen Hsi-shan and Feng Yu-hsiang which had been surrendered were moved southward to co-operate with their recent enemies, the Nanking forces, to face the common enemy. Offers of rewards for the capture of Communist leaders were made—unavailingly—and various attacks on their strongholds were begun.

[1] No. 2, p. 6.

Sporadic reports of sweeping victories, accompanied by the seizure of Communist lairs and the capture of Red leaders, have appeared in the press from time to time. They are strongly reminiscent, however, of reports to the throne in the nineteenth century of victories over the Taipings: the imperial forces always won, but the rebels seemed not to be aware of the fact. The Nationalist forces, too, are winning, but heaven is kind to the enemy. Like the imperial troops who fought the Taipings, the government troops are reported often to treat the people, on whom they are billeted, worse than the Communists treat them; this is not conducive to government victories. The government, if it has no other major wars to wage, and if it is able to put into effect its plans for national reconstruction upon which in recent months so much time and attention have been expended, may ultimately win by attrition. In the meantime, it is finding the ideology and the evanescence of the Communists a more difficult foe than were ever the old-time war lords or the perennial bandits. There appear to be involved in this struggle not merely personal ambitions and the desire for pelf, but also a conflict of political and social ideals which it is likely to take a very considerable time to harmonize. Until they are harmonized, or one side is completely crushed, the Chinese revolution cannot end, and no stability can be established.

CHAPTER XIII

CONCLUSION

THUS far an attempt has been made to explain the origins of the Chinese revolution, and to trace in some detail the political and military phases since 1911. For reasons stated in the Preface, the intricate relations existing between the foreign and the domestic problems involved have been generally avoided, but it should not be forgotten that the movements in progress have their origin as much outside the country as inside. For more than four hundred years the Chinese people have been increasingly affected by the influence of the West. Had it not been for this, and the problems arising out of the conflict between Western and Far Eastern civilizations, the struggle of the Chinese to overthrow the alien Manchu dynasty would, in all probability, have had no more serious or far-reaching results than earlier similar struggles on their part to demonstrate that heaven's mandate had been withdrawn from the ruling house. A period of confusion would have ended with the founding of another dynasty, and the country would have continued to swing in its ancient orbit.

The expulsion of the Manchus was a relatively simple matter; the attempt to institute a system of government essentially alien has proved more complicated. Even the unifying influence of a son of heaven, expressing the will of heaven and the reigning family through a hierarchy of scholar-officials, was never able definitively to overcome the physical and non-physical forces of decentralization eternally working in the Chinese world. After fourteen years of confusion the posthumous personality of Sun Yat-sen was substituted for that of the emperor, and, to a considerable degree, for that of Confucius. The portrait of the dead revolutionary leader, the conflicting ideology to be found in his writings, and a magnificent mausoleum at Nanking have not as yet sufficed to accomplish what the long line of dynasties, which ruled parts of the country from the dawn of history, never wholly succeeded in doing.

No people, however gifted, disciplined, and organized, can break completely with their past. That the Chinese are a gifted people no one can deny; but the degree to which they are disciplined and organized is subject to debate. Ability to coalesce temporarily for a negative purpose, such as a boycott or a strike, they have in a high degree, but union for advancement toward a positive goal, and willingness to sacrifice individual and family ambitions, and personal welfare, to follow a leader and a government for the good of the country as a whole are not as often to be observed. This, Yuan Shih-kai and Sun Yat-sen found during their troubled careers, and Chiang Kai-shek is still discovering.

Bearing in mind the ceaseless conflict of cultures through which the country is passing; the vast areas included in China and her far-flung dependencies; the civil wars, bandit raids, floods, earthquakes, famines, and pestilences from which the people suffer unendingly; the high percentage of illiteracy and general conservatism of the Chinese; the effect on their mind of their age-old

civilization, and the belief that their country constituted the center of the world, with themselves the only
civilized people therein, it is remarkable that as much
progress has been made in recent years as is to be
observed.

Yuan Shih-kai's generation of militarists has largely
passed into oblivion, to be succeeded, however, by a
fairly large and active group of younger and, apparently,
no less ambitious and selfish warriors. The military, as
well as the poor, China has always with her. Nevertheless, a system of government has been carefully worked
out on paper, and partly put into effect. This incorpo-
rates new and old elements, foreign and Chinese, which
may yet serve the country well. Model districts have
been, and are being, organized in several provinces to
serve as examples of administration for the surrounding
areas. Public parks, recreational centers, free schools,
and public libraries are being opened in considerable
numbers. The mass-education movement has obtained
a foothold in widely separated areas and, if foreign contributions continue until Chinese willingness to use their
own wealth for this purpose makes them no longer
necessary, much of good may come from it. Agriculture
and sericulture are being improved under both Chinese
and foreign leadership. Medical science, public health,
and hygiene are, likewise, being spread through the
country by the co-operation of Westerners with modern-
educated Chinese scientists. Irrigation, afforestation,
reforestation, and harbor projects are also being carried
out. New codes of law have been, and are still being,
promulgated which, in time, will be successfully applied
on a greater scale than at present; when this time comes

the militarists in control of a district, the local district committees of the Kuomingtang, and the central government itself will have ceased to interfere with the administration of justice for political purposes. Until the judiciary is independent, the number and modernity of codes of law are, of course, of small value except for propaganda purposes.

A generally efficient postal service, which grew out of the maritime-customs service under Sir Robert Hart's administration, is being maintained despite numerous difficulties. With the decision of England to remit the remainder of her Boxer indemnity funds, and to use a considerable part of these for railway construction in China, a great step forward may be taken in improvement of railway communications. Without such improvement, and the development of motor roads and waterways, the country can never be permanently unified administratively, and the ravages of famine and bandits prevented. In the construction of motor roads some progress is reported in almost every province, although at times the methods used for obtaining ground, funds, and labor for their construction have brought forth bitter protest and narrowly failed to cause revolt on the part of the hard-driven people. Such reforms as the ones mentioned, and many others which are being introduced, are often overlooked by critics of the military and political confusion from which the people are suffering.

Aside from the apparent inability of the people of China to unite whole-heartedly under discipline to follow a national leader, or government, the outstanding problems faced by contemporary China are those connected with the spread of communism, the lack of transportation, and the survival of militarism. The seriousness of the first has been discussed. With respect to the solution of the second a start has been made. Little, if any, real progress can be reported on the third. Lacking willingness on the part of the commanders and their troops to disband, and funds for so doing, as well as for the transfer of soldiers to constructive employment in civil life, the disbandment of the armies cannot take place. Without the removal of the burden of militarism from the country, sufficient funds are unavailable for the disbandment of the armies and the peaceful development of the country by the civil officials. Thus a vicious circle exists through which no politician has as yet been able to break to prove himself thereby a statesman of the first rank.

On May 4, the eve of the opening of the National People's Convention, the plans for the calling of which had caused a split between President Chiang Kai-shek and Mr. Hu Han-min, a new outbreak of the southern militarists occurred at Canton which illustrated anew the adage that, in May, Chinese generals' fancies lightly turn to thoughts of war. Under the partial instigation of Mr. Wang Ching-wei, who had recently returned to Hongkong from Europe, General Chen Chi-tang, who had gone to Nanking in January in company with Governor (and General) Huang Shao-hung of Kwangsi, to discuss the peaceful rehabilitation of the southern provinces, headed a revolt against President Chiang, and called upon him to resign his offices or fight to retain them. The quarrel with Hu, and the plan to promulgate a provisional constitution, were cited by Chiang's enemies as proofs of his plans to consolidate his position as dictator. Those in Canton who were loyal to Nanking were forced to flee, while plans were reported for a union with the former rebel generals of Kwangsi to be aided by the "Ironsides," the raising of an army of fifty thousand men to oust Chiang, the secession of the seven southern provinces, and the establishment of a new left-wing Kuomingtang government under Wang Ching-wei.

The arrival in Nanking by air of Marshal Chang Hsueh-liang to attend the Convention made it apparent that he was still loyal to the Nanking government, although there were intimations that some members of the government itself, including Mr. Sun Fo, were in sympathy with the southern rebel radicals.

The latest outbreak surprises no student of the revolution in China. It merely demonstrates that, despite the optimistic claims of Nanking to rule an already unified country, the old forces of decentralization, provincialism, and jealousy among the generals and politicians of any leader who presumes to lead, have not been overcome by the Kuomingtang national government conspicuously more successfully than they were by Yuan Shih-kai. It also shows that the fiery personality of Mr. Wang Ching-wei, who began his public career in 1909 by attempting to assassinate the prince regent, has, like that of Sun Yat-sen, not been quenched by the passage of years and numerous failures. Mr. Eugene Ch'en, the foreign minister of the Canton-Wuhan period of 1925–27 who retired abroad during the summer of 1927, returned to China in February, 1931. Two months later he was re-ensconced as a leader of the newly organized Canton government with which the aged T'ang Shao-yi affiliated himself. In June, Mr. C. C. Wu, Nanking's minister to Washington, resigned his post rather than constitute himself the channel of Nanking's appeal to the American government for arms with which to launch an attack on his home province.

Apparently as undaunted in May, 1931, as he was in March, 1929, on the occasion of the simultaneous outbreak of the Kwangsi faction at Wuhan and the opening of the Third Kuomingtang Congress, President Chiang opened the National People's Convention (Kuo-Min-Hui-I) on the fifth of the month, according to schedule.[1] While the members of the Convention listened to the reports of the progress and plans made by the national government, the President ordered troops to advance on Canton from Fukien province, commandeered Chinese vessels in Shanghai for purposes of transport, and ordered his minister of war, General Ho Ying-ch'in, to advance into Kiangsi to prevent co-operation between the southern rebels and the Communists. General Ho is a Kweichow man by birth, who distinguished himself by his loyalty to Chiang Kai-shek on the occasion of the latter's resignation of public office in the summer of 1927, and who had recently been stationed at Hankow directing the campaign against the Communists of South-Central China. If he now remains loyal to President Chiang and his government, and if Marshal Chang Hsueh-liang remains unshaken in his devotion to Nanking, it may be somewhat difficult for the Kwangtung-Kwangsi rebels to accomplish their aims. The widespread Communist movement in parts of their area and to the north of them, however, and

[1] For provisional constitution adopted by this Convention cf. Appendix.

the continued presence in the northwest of Marshal Feng, and the development of Moscow ideology in Shensi, are factors not to be lightly dismissed.

There is unlimited opportunity for criticism of the government of the Kuomingtang and its creature, the Nanking government. The honesty, sincerity, and ability of some of its participants may be debatable. That the country needs a strong government, with a carefully prepared program, is not, however, to be disputed by any impartial student of developments in China during the past century, and particularly during the past twenty years. The existing government is the best which republican China has yet evolved; it is doubtful if there exists in the country another group of men as capable as those which the Nanking branch of the Kuomingtang has succeeded in drawing to itself for purposes of administration. It is more than a little doubtful whether the overthrow of the existing group of men would be followed by the substitution of a more honest and capable assemblage. Rise to power has stabilized some of the earlier radicals, and, in the eyes of some, they have become conservative and autocratic. This appears to be characteristic of any group raised to power, and is not peculiar to the Chinese rulers at Nanking. The present shakeup may conceivably be stimulating to them and make them more careful, honest, and sincere in their attempts to rule a great people. Beyond this it is difficult to see that anything good can come from the latest attack of the southerners against Central and Northern China.

APPENDIX

CHINESE CONSTITUTION[1]

The following is the Yueh Fa (Provisional Constitution) as adopted at the fourth general session of the Kuo-Min-Hui-I (National People's Convention) on May 12, 1931:

PREAMBLE

The National Government, in order to reconstruct the Republic of China on the basis of the Three Principles of the People and the Constitution of Five Powers, which forms the underlying principle of the revolution, having now brought the revolution from the military to the political tutelage period, deems it necessary to promulgate a Yueh Fa (Provisional Constitution) for general observance, so that the realization of constitutional government may be accelerated and political power restored to a popularly-elected government; and further, in pursuance of the last will of our late Leader, has called at the national capital the Kuo-Min-Hui-I (National People's Convention).

The said National People's Convention do hereby enact and ordain the following Provisional Constitution for enforcement during the political tutelage period:

CHAPTER I. GENERAL PRINCIPLES

ARTICLE 1. The territory of the Republic of China consists of the various provinces and Mongolia and Tibet.

ART. 2. The sovereignty of the Republic of China is vested in the people as a whole.

All persons who, according to law, enjoy the nationality of the Republic of China shall be citizens (Kuo-Min) of the Republic of China.

ART. 3. The Republic of China shall be a unified republic forever.

[1] From the *North China Herald*, Vol. CLXXIX, No. 3328 (May 19, 1931), p. 221.

ART. 4. The national flag of the Republic of China shall have a red background with a "blue sky and white sun" in the upper left corner.

ART. 5. Nanking shall be the national Capital of the Republic of China.

CHAPTER II. RIGHTS AND DUTIES OF THE PEOPLE

ART. 6. All citizens (Kuo-Min) of the Republic of China shall be equal before the law, irrespective of sex, race, religion or caste.

ART. 7. Citizens of the Republic of China shall, according to the stipulation of Article 8 of the "Outline of National Reconstruction," enjoy in all completely autonomous districts (Hsien) the rights of election, initiative, recall and referendum as provided by Article 9 of the "Outline of National Reconstruction."

ART. 8. Except in accordance with law, no person (Jen-min) shall be arrested, detained, tried or punished.

When a person is arrested or detained on a criminal charge, the organ responsible for his (or her) arrest or detention shall send him (or her) to the competent court for trial not later than 24 hours. The party concerned may himself petition, or some other person may petition on his behalf, that he be brought (before the Court) for trial within 24 hours.

ART. 9. Except in accordance with law, no person other than those in active military service shall be subject to trial by a military court.

ART. 10. Except in accordance with law, no private houses of the people shall be subject to forcible entry, search or sealing.

ART. 11. All persons shall have the liberty of conscience.

ART. 12. All persons shall be free to choose and change their residence; such freedom shall not be denied or restricted except in accordance with law.

ART. 13. All persons shall have the right to the privacy of correspondence and telegraphic communications: such right shall not be denied or restricted except in accordance with law.

ART. 14. All persons shall have the freedom of assembly and formation of associations: such freedom shall not be denied or restricted except in accordance with law.

ART. 15. All persons shall have the liberty of speech and publication: such liberty shall not be denied or restricted except in accordance with law.

ART. 16. Except in accordance with law, no private property shall be sealed or confiscated.

Art. 17. The exercise of the right of ownership by any private owner of property, in so far as it does not conflict with the public interest, shall be protected by law.

Art. 18. Where public interest necessitates, the property of the people may be expropriated in accordance with law.

Art. 19. All persons shall have the right to inherit property in accordance with law.

Art. 20. All persons shall have the right of petition (to the Government).

Art. 21. All persons shall have the right to institute judicial proceedings at the courts of justice, in accordance with law.

Art. 22. All persons shall have the right to submit petitions, and institute administrative proceedings (at the Administrative Court) in accordance with law (for the redress of wrongs done by Government administrative organs).

Art. 23. All persons shall have the right to compete in civil service examinations in accordance with law.

Art. 24. All persons may, according to law, hold public posts.

Art. 25. All persons shall have the duty of paying taxes in accordance with law.

Art. 26. All persons shall have the duty of undertaking military service and of performing compulsory labour (for the state) in accordance with law.

Art. 27. All persons shall have the duty to obey the measures taken by Government Organs in the performance of their duties according to law.

Chapter III. Essentials of Political Tutelage

Art. 28. The political policies and programs during the period of political tutelage shall be in accordance with the "Outline of National Reconstruction."

Art. 29. The system of district autonomy shall be enforced in accordance with the provisions of the "Outline of National Reconstruction" and the "Law Governing the Institution of District Autonomy."

Art. 30. During the period of political tutelage, the National Congress of Kuomintang delegates (Kuo-Min-Tang-Tsuan-Kuo-Tai-Piao Ta-Hui) shall exercise the governing powers on behalf of the National People's Congress (Kuo-Min-Ta-Hui). During the recess of the National Congress of Kuomintang delegates, the Central Executive Committee of the Kuomintang shall exercise the said powers.

Art. 31. The National Government shall train and guide (the citizens) in the exercise of the four political rights of election, initiative, recall and referendum.

Art. 32. The National Government shall exercise the five governing powers, namely, executive, legislative, judicial, examination and supervisory.

Chapter IV. People's Livelihood

Art. 33. In order to develop the people's economic welfare, the state (Kuo-Chia) shall afford every encouragement and protection to the productive enterprises of the people.

Art. 34. In order to develop rural economy, to improve the living conditions of farmers as well as to promote the well-being of peasants, the state shall take active steps for the carrying out of the following measures:

1. Reclamation of all waste land in the country and development of farm irrigation;
2. Establishment of agricultural banks and encouragement of cooperative enterprises in the rural communities;
3. Enforcement of the (public) granary system for the prevention of famine and other calamities and replenishment of the people's food supplies;
4. Development of agricultural education with special emphasis on scientific experiments, extensive development of agricultural enterprises and increase of agricultural produce.
5. Encouragement of road-building in the rural villages to facilitate the transportation of agricultural products.

Art. 35. The state shall open and develop oil, coal, gold and iron mines; and shall also encourage and protect private mining enterprises.

Art. 36. The state shall undertake and inaugurate state shipping enterprises; and shall also encourage and protect private shipping enterprises.

Art. 37. All persons shall be free to choose their profession or occupation. But when it is contrary to the public interest, the state may, by law, restrict or deny such freedom.

Art. 38. All persons shall be free to make contracts: such freedom, in so far as it is not in conflict with the public interest or with good morals, shall be protected by law.

ART. 39. In order to better their economic well-being as well as to promote closer co-operation between Capital and Labour, the people may form occupational organizations in accordance with law.

ART. 40. Both capital and labour shall develop productive enterprises in accordance with the principle of co-operation and mutual benefit.

ART. 41. In order to improve the living conditions of labour, the state shall put into effect various laws for the protection of labour and shall afford special protection to child and woman workers in respect to their age and health.

ART. 42. In order to safeguard as well as relieve peasants and workers who shall be unable to work on account of accidents, sickness, disability or old age, the state shall put into effect a labour insurance system.

ART. 43. In order to promote the economic interests of the people, the state shall encourage and promote various co-operative enterprises.

ART. 44. The state may control or regulate the production or sale as well as the market price of daily necessaries of the people.

ART. 45. Laws shall be enacted for the prohibition of usury, and exorbitant rents for the use of immovable properties.

ART. 46. The state shall give appropriate relief to those members of the national forces who are disabled in the course of active service.

Chapter V. Education of the Citizens

ART. 47. The Three Principles of the People shall be the basic principles of education in the Republic of China.

ART. 48. Both sexes shall have equal opportunity for education.

ART. 49. All public and private educational institutions in the country shall be subject to the supervision of the state, and shall also be responsible for the carrying out of the educational policies adopted by the state.

ART. 50. All children of school age shall receive free education. Details shall be separately provided by law.

ART. 51. Those who have not had free education (in their youth) shall receive special adult education. Details shall be separately provided by law.

ART. 52. The Central and Local Governments shall provide adequate funds for necessary educational expenses, and shall also safeguard the security of funds which are, by law, specially set apart (for educational purposes).

Art. 53. The state shall give encouragement or grants to private educational institutions which have achieved particularly satisfactory results.

Art. 54. Encouragement and grants shall be given for the education of overseas Chinese.

Art. 55. The state shall encourage and safeguard members of the administrative or teaching staffs of schools who hold satisfactory records and have been long in service.

Art. 56. All public and private educational institutions in the country shall establish scholarships and prizes for the encouragement of deserving but needy students.

Art. 57. The state shall encourage and protect research and discoveries in science or the arts.

Art. 58. The state shall protect and preserve historic remains and ancient relics which have historical, cultural or artistic value.

CHAPTER VI. DIVISION OF POWER BETWEEN THE
CENTRAL AND LOCAL GOVERNMENTS

Art. 59. The principle of equilibrium shall be adopted in the division of power between the Central and Local Governments, as stipulated in Article 17 of the "Outline of National Reconstruction."

Art. 60. The various local governments may, within their respective sphere of authority, enact and ordain local laws and regulations. Where such laws and regulations are in conflict with those promulgated by the Central Government, they shall be null and void.

Art. 61. The demarcation of central and local revenues shall be separately determined by law.

Art. 62. The Central Government may restrict, by law, any local tax when

1. It is contrary to public interest,
2. It encroaches upon the source of central revenue,
3. It constitutes overlapping taxation,
4. It is detrimental to communications,
5. It is unjustifiably imposed upon goods imported from other localities for the sole benefit of the locality concerned,
6. It is in the nature of a transit duty on commodities in circulation among various localities.

Art. 63. The power of granting patents and monopolies is vested in the Central Government.

Art. 64. When one of the provinces reaches the period of Constitutionalism, the division of power between the central and the Local Governments shall be defined in detail by law in accordance with the "Outline of National Reconstruction."

Chapter VII. Organization of the Governments

SECTION I. THE CENTRAL GOVERNMENT

Art. 65. The National Government shall exercise all the governing powers of the Republic of China.

Art. 66. The National Government shall have supreme command over the land, naval and air forces.

Art. 67. The National Government shall have the power to declare war, to negotiate peace and to conclude treaties.

Art. 68. The National Government shall exercise the power of granting amnesties, pardons, reprieves and restitution of civic rights.

Art. 69. The National Government shall exercise the power of conferring medals and decorations of honor.

Art. 70. The National Government shall compile and publish a budget and financial statement of the national revenues and expenditures for each fiscal year.

Art. 71. The National Government shall be composed of the following five Yuan: the Executive Yuan, the Legislative Yuan, the Judicial Yuan, the Examination Yuan and the Control Yuan, as well as various Ministries and Commissions.

Art. 72. The National Government shall have a President and an appropriate number of State Councillors, who shall be selected and appointed by the Central Executive Committee of the Kuomintang. The number of State Councillors shall be separately determined by law.

Art. 73. The President of the National Government shall represent the National Government both internally and internationally.

Art. 74. The Presidents of the five Yuan and the Heads of the various Ministries and Commissions shall be appointed or dismissed in accordance with law by the National Government at the instance of the President of the National Government.

Art. 75. All laws shall be promulgated and Mandates issued upon the signature of the President of the National Government according to law.

Art. 76. The various Yuan, Ministries or Commissions may, according to law, issue orders.

Art. 77. The organization of the National Government and of the various Yuan, Ministries and Commissions shall be separately determined by law.

SECTION 2. THE LOCAL GOVERNMENT

Art. 78. In each province, a Provincial Government shall be established, which shall attend to the administration of provincial affairs under the direction of the National Government. Its organization shall be separately determined by law.

Art. 79. When, as stipulated in Article 16 of the "Outline of National Reconstruction," a province reaches the period of Constitutionalism, the (Provincial) Assembly of People's Delegates may elect a Provincial Governor (Sheng-Chang).

Art. 80. The system of local government in Mongolia and Tibet shall be determined separately by law in the light of the local conditions.

Art. 81. In each district (Hsien), a District Government shall be established, which shall attend to the administration of district affairs under the direction of the Provincial Governments. Its organization shall be separately determined by law.

Art. 82. In each of the districts, a district autonomy preparatory committee shall be organized to carry out the preparations as provided for in Article 8 of the "Outline of National Reconstruction." Its organization shall be separately determined by law.

Art. 83. Municipalities may be established in localities where industry and commerce, population or other special conditions warrant. The organization of such Municipalities shall be separately determined by Law.

CHAPTER VIII. ANNEX

Art. 84. All laws which are in conflict with this Yueh Fa (Provisional Constitution) shall be null and void.

Art. 85. The power of interpreting this Yueh Fa shall be exercised by the Central Executive Committee of the Kuomintang of China.

Art. 86. A draft of the (Permanent) Constitution (Hsien Fa) shall be prepared by the Legislative Yuan on the basis of the "Outline of National Reconstruction" as well as the achievements during the political tutelage and constitutional periods. The said draft shall be duly made known to the people at large in preparation for its adoption and enforcement at the opportune moment.

ART. 87. When a majority of the provinces in the country reach the period of Constitutionalism—that is, when district autonomy has been completely instituted throughout each of such provinces—then the National Government shall immediately summon a National People's Congress (Kuo-Min-Ta-Hui) to decide upon the adoption and promulgation of the Hsien Fa (Permanent Constitution).

ART. 88. The present Yueh Fa (Provisional Constitution) shall be enacted by the National People's Convention (Kuo-Min-Hui-I) and forwarded to the National Government for promulgation.

ART. 89. The present Yueh Fa shall come into force from the date of promulgation.

INDEX

237